LAST
WORD

LAST WORD

A Charity Anthology to Benefit Nation Inside

www.nationinside.org

JOYRIDE PRESS

Book and interior design by Hugh Wilson.

ISBN-13: 978-0-9908669-1-6

For purchasing information, please visit www. joyridepressbooks.com

Table of Contents

Foreward

The stories you are about to read are about criminals, for the most part. When I started out, I wanted to find ten of the best short story writers I knew, and get a contribution from each. What I found, as I was reading each story, was a recurrent theme: desperation. There are ten different stories, and ten different perspectives and voices, some eccentric, some comical, and some downright raw, but I found the protagonists were driven by their circumstances.

I chose the first story because it showed the dual nature of a criminal; being held back from meaningful opportunity after being released from prison, and the urge to fall back into old habits. Few crime writers write about the aftermath of crime. The incarceration. The violence in our prison system that can turn non-violent offenders into violent offenders as a matter of survival. A parole system that is overworked and understaffed. The inability to get a job to match your skill because you have a record. And in the case of war, the injustice and inhumanity of imprisonment without charge.

For these reasons, the full proceeds of this book will go to the Nation Inside organization, a coordinating organization that unites national efforts to pass prison reform measures.

About the title... I originally meant for this book to last, and to that end, copies of this ebook, PDF and text file will be transcribed to a new, non-metallic media that, if not physically crushed, is rated to last one-thousand, three hundred years. So no matter what happens to publishing, there will at least be a chance that this book will be unearthed long after we're all dead. So yeah, we'll have the last word.

I'd like to thank Dave Jaggers, Steve Weddle, Todd Robinson, Jack Getze, Court Merrigan, Gareth Spark, Les Edgerton, Tess Makovesky, Angel Luis Colon and Christopher Pimental for their last words.

Liam Sweeny

Editor

A Dark Ride

David Jaggers

She was absolutely beautiful, and the last thing I needed in my life. I first saw her when I stepped out back of the restaurant to grab a quick smoke before my shift started. She was parked across the street, a low-slung vision in black. She was a 1969 Dodge Charger special edition and she was cherry. I could get ten grand for a car like that; more than half of what I make in a year washing dishes. Boosting that ride would set me and Debbie up, get us and the kid out of her mother's house. Problem was, I don't steal cars no more. Three years upstate put an end to that. Little Jillian was a baby when I went in and I just can't risk goin back. I'd lose them both.

"Goddammit Nick! We're outta glasses and forks again. What the fuck are you doin back here, pullin your dick?"

I took a deep breath of garbage filled steam and shrugged. "Sorry Harry, the machine keeps jammin up, I think the conveyor's broken again."

"I don't pay you to think Nick, I pay you to keep my fucking dishes clean. I got customers who want to eat and no goddamned silverware. Make it happen or your ass is on the street."

Harry was a real asshole but he was the only guy who'd give me a job when I got out. I really wanted to tell him to shove it, but instead I shoved the plastic rack of drinking glasses into the open mouth of the dish machine. I grabbed a bus tub from the stack and headed out into the dining area to clean the empty tables. It was the same scene every day, a few tourists taking bites of their burgers between glances at landmark pamphlets, and the two or three regulars that came in daily.

I swept the empty plates and coffee mugs into the tub and used a bleach soaked rag to wipe the tables down. I walked past the one regular who held court in the booth nearest the door. I remembered him because he was a short bald man and had a strange habit of arranging his dishes in neat rows, with the fork and knife perfectly lined up next to his napkin which he folded into a precise square. This guy must've had some kind of mental problem, because he came in every single day and spent at least an hour at the booth working a crossword puzzle and aligning his utensils.

My shift ended at three, after the lunch rush was over and all the prep dishes from the morning were cleaned. I tossed my filthy apron into the pile and stepped out the back door into the fresh air. My lungs were screaming for a smoke and an escape from the humid hell of the diner's dish room. As I put on my jacket I saw her again. The black paint and that long, slick chassis drew my attention like a tight ass in a skirt.

All I could think of was the adrenaline rush I'd feel when I sparked the wires and fired her up for the first time. The fear of being caught, the smell of the money. It was an addiction.

When I was in my prime I never messed with cars like her. She was too flashy, too unique to turn a quick buck. I always went for the sedans, the Accords and Camrys, something that could be chopped up quick and not turn heads when I drove it down the street. But, there was just something about that car that dug into my mind and wouldn't let go. I laid awake that night thinking about her, thinking about my buddy Joey who had the connection upstate and could move her quick and clean, thinking about the ten grand and my little family. I didn't want to go back to prison, but the grind of catching the bus to wash dishes and living in Debbie's mom's basement was tearing at me.

I had pretty much decided when I woke up that if she was out there the next day, I was gonna take her. I dug out Joey's number and called him before my shift started.

"No shit, a 69? It'll take me a while to find a buyer, but I can definitely turn it. Damn man it's like old times. You was always one of my favorites."

"Well this is a one-time thing Joey. Just this one score. I really need the money."

"Yeah sure buddy. Whatever you say. Just drop it off at the old garage out by the water treatment plant, you remember the drill?"

"Yeah, I remember. Just have somebody waiting to take me back into town. Hey thanks again Joey and seriously this is the only one."

I hung up the pay phone and pressed my forehead against

the cold metal coin slot. I couldn't believe I was doing this again. I could feel the old me seeping through the cracks of this new life. The life that I had tried to build after prison. I walked around the block to the restaurant and felt my heartbeat quicken when I saw her parked against the curb, crouched like a black tiger waiting to lunge at an unsuspecting meal.

My shift felt like it lasted forever. Harry was on my ass the entire time about the busted garbage compactor and the place was packed. Crossword puzzle man stayed longer than usual and I had to wait until he left to clean the booth. When I finally got out, it was a quarter till four. My heart almost stopped when I walked around the dumpster and she wasn't there, but the panic faded when I noticed she had been moved down a few spaces. I was pretty sure the owner lived in the two-story walk up across from the restaurant, but I had never seen anybody get in or out of the car. Whoever he was, he kept to himself.

The real key to stealing a car is speed. It don't matter if it has a fancy alarm, or even if it's out in the open. A good car thief can be in and gone in under a minute. I could do it in thirty seconds. I walked up to the car and did a quick scan to see if anybody was looking, when I was satisfied that I had my chance, I pulled the slim Jim from my jacket and slid it between the glass and the chrome on the driver's door. Within seconds I was in and had the door closed. The car was just as clean and polished on the inside as the exterior. Detailed to perfection. I leaned across the leather seat and worked the wires loose under the steering column. A couple of sparks flew, and that old adrenaline rush came over me.

The engine growled to life and I quickly slammed it into gear and took off. I looked at my watch, forty seconds. Damn I was out of practice.

The next few days felt like a dream. I stuck to my normal routine, work and home, but inside I was a different man. For the first time in forever, I had prospects. Things were looking up. On Friday I stopped by the payphone and rang Joey's number. I was supposed to check in and find out when I was going to get paid. He didn't answer, which wasn't like him, but I blew it off and went on in to work. I figured I'd try him again after my shift. The restaurant was dead, not even Mr. Crossword came in, so Harry let me leave a little early and I went straight to the phone and dialed Joey's number. No answer. I started having this feeling that Joey might be trying to stiff me, so I called Debbie and told her I'd picked up a half shift and wouldn't be home for a while. I took the bus across town and walked the remaining three blocks to the old garage.

The place was dark and quiet when I walked up, which was odd cause Joey always had at least two mechanics chopping down cars at any given time. The side door was unlocked so I let myself in. One of the garage bays was empty and the other had a late-model BMW up on blocks. There was no sign of the Charger. I walked over to the little office that Joey kept in the back, it wasn't much bigger than a closet with just enough room to hold a desk and a grease smeared computer. I opened the door and was hit in the face with the hot, metallic stench of blood. I screamed when I saw what was left of Joey, slumped over in the corner. The skin on his face had been peeled off and his lips were missing. His bulging eyes stared toward the door like he wanted to get up and run. I backed up and nearly fell over a small tool box behind me. I stifled my gag reflex, grabbed an oily rag from the floor and wiped my prints off the doorknob. I noticed a small piece of paper, soaked in blood on Joey's desk. It was the number to the payphone by the diner.

A cold fear washed over me, and I couldn't bear to be in the garage any longer. I ran out the back door and screamed again when I saw the two mechanics hanging from an engine hoist, their throats were cut and blood dripped from their boots, pooling on the ground below. I jumped the small fence that ringed the parts yard and ran all the way back to the bus stop.

†††

"What's wrong with you Nick, you're so jumpy?" Debbie said over the plate of microwave lasagna.

"Nothing baby, work has been stressful. Harry's been on my ass more than usual, that's all. Why don't we take a few days and go visit your aunt in Atlantic City? Jilly Bean would love to see the boardwalk, right?"

Debbie dropped her fork on the plate. "Nick, what's going on? You don't ever talk about going anywhere unless there's some trouble. You promised me you'd stay straight."

"It's nothing like that baby. Things have just been so hard lately. Living here with your mom and all. I figure a change of scenery would do us some good."

"We're lucky she took us in Nick. Where else were we gonna go huh? Besides we don't have the money to go to Atlantic City. You barely make enough to cover the bills. Stop that crazy talk, you're worrying me."

After Debbie and Jillian were asleep I got up and quietly pulled the refrigerator out from the wall and grabbed the 9mm I had taped to the back. It was a violation of my parole to have a gun, but I never left myself without protection. I tucked the pistol into my pants and stepped outside the basement apartment for a smoke. Somewhere out there, the Charger's owner was looking for me. I didn't know what Joey told him, but I imagined he talked plenty under the edge of that knife. Joey didn't know where I lived, or worked, all he knew was the number I called from.

My heart nearly beat out of my chest as I walked to the diner the next day. From the moment I stepped off the bus, and walked the block to the restaurant's side door, I felt like there were crosshairs trained on me in the distance. The skin on the back of my neck prickled. I rang the bell on the back door and waited for Harry to let me in. After a minute I pushed it again, sometimes Harry was up front and didn't hear the buzzer. Finally the deadbolt clicked and I pulled the door open. Harry had a bag of onions in one hand and a large knife in the other.

"Get the fuck in here Nick, we got a call this morning from the bank across the street, they want ten box lunches. I'm up to my elbows in Caesar salads right now."

I grabbed a fresh apron from the folded stack and started the process of firing up the dish machine. Soon I was in the groove and had almost forgotten about the events of the night before. After the morning routine of cleaning the prep utensils, I grabbed the bus tub and headed out front. The place was hopping, and only one table was empty, the one next to crossword puzzle man. I sat my tub town on the chair and began to remove the plates. The bald man looked up from his perfectly arranged table and spoke.

††††

"Hey kid, I'm stuck on this one clue, maybe you can help me. What's an eight letter word for a car thief's destination? Oh wait a minute I got it. Chopshop."

I froze in place, my pulse throbbing in my skull. I looked up at the small bald man, his cold stare cut right through me. He flipped through to the back of his puzzle book and pulled out a Polaroid picture. He put it on the table so I could see it. It was a snapshot of Debbie and Jillian, taken that morning on their way to school.

The bald man sipped his coffee and smiled. "It rips a man's heart out to lose his prize possession don't you agree?"

I stood perfectly still, staring at the picture. I could hear Harry's voice in the background yelling at me to get moving, but it was distant and foggy. I thought about the pistol I had in my jacket, but that was in the back room and there was no time to grab it. Finally I spoke.

"What do I need to do to keep them safe?

The bald man replaced his coffee mug and carefully adjusted the handle so it pointed squarely to the right. He closed his crossword book and stuffed it in his jacket pocket.

"You take a ride with me and I promise they'll be just fine.

Meet me out back in five minutes. And kid, leave the pistol here."

I felt like someone had punched me in the gut. I took the bus tub to the back and ignored Harry as he screamed at me for slacking off. I took off my apron and hung it from the peg on the dish machine.

"Sorry Harry, I quit."

"What? You sorry sack of shit, you gonna leave me hangin right in the middle of your shift? I knew you was trouble. Fucking ex-cons."

I opened the backdoor and walked out onto the little concrete pad that held the dumpster. I lit a cigarette and inhaled deeply. The sun was out and there was a light breeze carrying the aroma of last night's trash. I walked around the corner and saw her sitting there. A black shadow accented in chrome. She was idling and I could feel the rumble in my guts. As I crossed the street, I could see the bald man behind the wheel. I flicked the cig to the pavement and pulled the handle on the passenger door. As we pulled out, I couldn't help but think that she was still the most beautiful car I had ever seen.

J. David Jaggers lives in fly over country, where he spends his days in the white collar world and his nights feeding the thugs, pimps, and enforcers he keeps caged in his basement. He has been published in Near to the Knuckle, Yellow Mama, Spelk, Out of the Gutter and various other magazines and anthologies.

The Luck Of The Devil

Paul D. Brazill

Toby Richards was sobbing like a scalded child. Begging forgiveness. Whimpering and whining, as usual. He was blindfolded, and naked, face down on Ania Nowak's four-poster bed. The whip marks on his flabby back and chubby buttocks were still red. Ania had been venomously insulting him for the last hour or so and was getting hoarse. Getting bored.

She stood over him, dressed in black leather, her lipstick blood-red, her blonde hair short-cropped. High-heels accentuating her long muscular legs. She wished the asshole would hurry up and spill his seed so that she could get rid of him and have a drink. She really needed a jolt but Toby was one of those twelve step losers and he'd freak if he smelt a trace of booze on her breath. Especially so early in the morning. As she finished whipping his ass, Ania wondered if she were the higher force that they talked about at his AA meetings, but doubted it.

Still, he was a successful film director and he certainly paid
well enough. He was visiting her more and more regularly
these days, too and her little nest egg wasn't so little any more.
She turned the whip around, coated the handle in KY jelly
and slowly inserted it into Toby's anus. She blanked out his
screams and looked out of her window as a firework exploded
and filled the early dawn sky with a cascade of colours. At
the same moment, Toby made a familiar, pathetic whining
sound. She slowly eased the whip out of his backside and
placed it in a black bin liner.

'Okey dokey?' she whispered.

Toby grunted.

She went over to the television and switched it on. Sat in
front of it watching 'Lovejoy' as Toby shuffled off, shame-
faced, to the bathroom.

She heard the shower run and Toby scream with pain.
Grinned for a moment and then got tired of his whining.
Tried to concentrate on Ian McShane's latest scam. A few
minutes later, Toby came out of the bathroom, dressed quickly
in jeans and a hoodie and left, closing the door carefully and
as quietly as possible.

Ania went over to the bedside table and saw her money
and a packet of white powder. Toby was one of the increasing
few of her regular clients who paid in cash these days, which
suited her. Her last tax bill had been massive and she typically
wondered who actually was screwing her. She walked over to
the drinks cabinet and poured a large Jack Daniels. Filled the
rest of the glass with Pepsi. Drank it down. Looked at the
money. Felt good very quickly. Looked at the money again.
Poured another drink. Breakfast of champions.

†††

Trevor's hot breath appeared and disappeared on the cold windowpane like a spectre. He couldn't help smiling as he watched his kids make a snowman in the park outside. Sindy, their dog barked at them while his wife Sarah drank coffee from a tartan thermos flask. They waved and headed off across the park.

Trevor Malone felt calm for a moment. Contented. It didn't last long, though. He looked at his Rolex and his agitation returned. He turned and glared at Bernie.

'Where is fuck he, then? Answer me that. Where is the tosser? You know, some of us have better things to do, eh?' said Trevor.

Trevor had been doing his best to keep calm, he really had. But is it was particularly hard there in Bernie's office, what with the heating being switched off as usual. He had turned up the collar on his Crombie and put his flat cap and leather gloves back on but he was still freezing his nads off.

Big Bernie Carr, on the other hand, had taken off his jacket, loosened his tie and rolled up his sleeves. He was knocking back the Evian and dabbing his forehead with a paper towel. Semi circles of sweat around each armpit. Looking like a reject from Miami Vice in his powder blue linen suit and salmon pink shirt.

'I have no idea where he is, Trev, I'm not my brother's keeper,' said Bernie.

'He needs a keeper, your Wurzel does,' said Trevor. 'One with a very big stick and a bigger cage.'

He stamped his feet on the concrete floor.

'True enough. Monkey Boy's been a liability for as long as I can remember but family's family,' said Bernie. 'Blood's thicker than water.'

'Yeah, but money's thicker than blood,' said Trevor. 'Especially the sort of money we're talking about.'

Bernie snorted. He walked over to a globe shaped drinks cabinet in the corner of the half-decorated office and opened it up.

'Too late for a snifter? Or too early?' he said.

'Why not,' said Trevor, 'it might warm me up.'

Bernie grinned and made himself a gin and tonic. He poured Trevor a double Maker's Mark.

'I take it you won't be wanting ice,' he said. Guffawed as he passed the drink to Trevor.

'You're a droll fucker, Bernie,' said Trevor. 'Always have been. Even at school you were a lippy twat.'

'Best years of our lives, those, eh?'

He took a long, slow drink.

'Naw, it was shite,' said Trevor.

'Aye, you're right. Torture. If I had my time over again I'd ...'

There was a loud bang against the office door and it slowly creaked open, scraping against the concrete floor.

††††

The doorbell rang and Ania roused herself from her morning nap. She looked through the spyhole. Opened the door.

'Early as always, kochanie,' said Ania.

'Bad habits are hard to break,' said Tina. She walked into

the room with two clinking Waitrose bags filled with wine and plonked them on the table as Ania switched off the television.

'Tracey Chapman okay for you?' said Ania, flicking through her CD collection.

'Fine by me. I'm feeling a little mellow. Just had a snifter in The Tea Clipper.'

Ania looked at her watch. Saw that it was almost noon.

'Anyone interesting in there?' said Ania. She took off her leather garb and pulled on a red kimono.

Tina opened a bottle of wine and filled two large glasses.

'Just the usual boring old farts. Expect for Pablo, of course.' She licked her lips.

'I'm surprised he's still here in London,' said Ania, frowning. 'He's playing with fire hanging around so long. If Boris finds out …'

She ran a finger across her throat.

'He likes risk, as you know,' said Tina. 'That's part of his appeal. And you know what they say: if you don't risk you don't drink champagne.'

'I'll stick with the wine, thanks,' said Ania.

They both collapsed onto her sofa.

'So, what's the story? What's this great news you're desperate to share with me?'

'I'll tell you later,' said Tina. 'I need to wind down.'

She leaned over and kissed Ania.

'Come on, luv,' she said. 'Not in the mood?'

'I'm getting there,' said Ania with a smirk.

She stood and led Tina over to the bed.

'I haven't changed the sheets,' said Ania. 'Are you okay

with that?'

Tina pushed her down onto the bed.

'I'll take that as a yes,' said Ania.

†††

'Speak of the devil,' said Bernie.

Wurzel Carr shuffled into the room. His eyes and nose were red. He was tall, wiry. Had a dishevelled beard and wore a crumpled charity shop tweed suit. Scuffed brogues. He looked like a living Scarecrow. Always had. Hence the nickname.

'Jesus, Wurzel, you look like shite. Even by your particularly low standards,' said Trevor.

Wurzel plucked a pin sized roll up from his bottom lip. Smirked.

'Seen better days, aye,' he rasped. 'But haven't had better nights, I can tell you.'

He winked and collapsed into a leather armchair that was still covered in cellophane. Held out a hand, clicked his fingers.

Bernie frowned and went to the mini-bar and filled a half pint glass with vodka. Handed it to Wurzel, who took a swig. Licked his lips.

'Breakfast of champions,' said Trevor.

Wurzel looked him up and down.

'Pots and kettles, Trev?' he said.

Trevor looked at the half empty glass of whisky in his hand.

'When in Rome,' he said.

Bernie topped up Trevor's glass.

'Here's a bit more spaghetti.'

Trevor sighed as he sat down on the edge of Bernie's desk.

'You got the clobber, then?' he said to Wurzel.

'Trevor, Trevor. Clever Trevor. Ye of little faith. I'm hurt that you even need to ask me that,' said Wurzel.

Trevor stood up. Loomed over Wurzel.

'Well?'

'Patience is a virtue, Trevor. You should try to be a bit more Zen. It'll help your blood pressure.'

'I'll stick your Zen up your arse and your Ying and Tang after it if you don't ...'

'It's Yin and Yang actually. A common ...'

'Wurzel!' barked Bernie. 'He got to his feet. 'Stop pissing about.'

Wurzel licked his ragged moustache.

'Alright, alright. Hold your arses.'

He carefully put his glass on the floor and unsteadily stood up. Made a show of stretching his muscles.

Trevor started to chew the inside of his cheek.

Wurzel pushed a hand into his jacket inside pocket. Plucked out a small oval shaped package and held it aloft.

'Ta dah! Viola, cello, banjo, whatever tickles your fancy,' he said.

'You sure that's the real Totenkopfring?' said Trevor.

'For sure, Trev. The real deal, the real I am, bona fide ...'

He put it on Bernie's desk. Bernie opened the box to reveal a ring with a skull and crossbones design

'You know, Himmler gave SS honour rings to lots of members of the Old Guard. How do we know it's actually his personal skull ring?' said Trevor.

'I've had it checked out, authenticated,' said Wurzel.

He handed an envelope to Trevor.

'All the info's in there, like.'

'So, that's our side of the bargain, Trevor,' said Bernie. 'Now it's your turn'

Trevor picked up his briefcase from the corner of the room and put it on the desk, keeping an eye on the package as he did. He clicked it up and took out two large bundles.

'There you go,' he said. He handed on to Bernie and one to Wurzel. 'Fifty-fifty. Same as usual?'

'Share and share alike, that's us,' said Wurzel.

Trevor picked up the package. Peeled back the gaudy wrapping paper. A grin crawled across his face like a caterpillar. He put it in his briefcase and clicked it shut.

'Right, I'm off to meet the wife in some twee café over Chiswick. Got to spend the afternoon traipsing around Horrids with her and the kids,' he said.

'Going to practice your Russian, eh?' said Wurzel. He polished off his drink, started flicking though the cash.

'And don't I know it,' said Trevor. 'No peace for the wicked.'

He put his hands in his coat pockets and pulled out two guns.

'Still, we all have our own double-cross to bear,' he said as he blasted Wurzel and Bernie in the face.

†††

Tina wiped the cappuccino froth from her top lip, carefully avoiding smudging her lipstick. She looked longingly out of the crowded café's window at the glowing womb like pub on the opposite side of the road. Night was quickly melting into day and the street's flickering Christmas lights were reflected in the wet pavement. Chiswick High Road was bustling. Stressed out shoppers rushed by babbling into smartphones. A drunken Santa pissed against a clamped BMW, a kebab held aloft to the evening drizzle. A black cab skidded onto the pavement and a drunken fat woman with a plastic Christmas tree staggered out of the passenger seat and fell into the gutter.

Tina caught her reflection in the window.

'God, I look knackered, I really do. Old. Ancient. I wonder if old age is catching?' she said.

Ania laughed.

Tina looked at Ania Nowak. Tall, blonde, late-twenties and full of herself. She was smirking. A told you so on the tip of her dainty but sharp tongue.

'You're becoming paranoid. Too much of the marching powder up your nose, kochania,' said Ania.

'Pots and kettles!'

'I don't own a kettle and certainly not a pot,' said Ania.

'I'm serious. I even found a grey hair in my comb the other morning and attacked the hair dye so much it took me all day to clean my hands. Made sure I didn't miss a bit. I really hate that salt and pepper thing, reminds me of my bloody mother. I blame Sebastian, I do. It's all his fault. He's put years on me since I married him.'

'He's really so bad?' said Ania.

'He is! I've pretty much reached the end of my tether. I've just about had enough of Sebastian's obsessions. His rants. His moaning. His petty gripes. The whole grumpy old man act. It was funny once upon a time, when we were sat in La Salsa a few sheets to the wind. Coked up. But since I moved in with him, I realised that he's actually like that all the time. And the joke isn't funny anymore, like that bloody awful song he keeps playing. If it's not his bloody depressing music taste, it's the crap old comedy DVDs that he plays over and over again, ad infinitum. The look of disapproval on his face when I don't laugh at the same tired catchphrase that has been repeated over and over again like a stuck record. I never thought I'd crack so quickly,' she said. 'Six bloody months and I'm ready to slash my wrists and his throat.'

'He's more than twenty years older than you. You can't expect to like the same things,' said Ania, her cut-glass accent actually sharp enough to slit Sebastian's throat. 'Differences are to be expected. And, you know, kochanie, domestic drudgery isn't for everyone. It really isn't you is it? And now you know there are good reasons why it's not advisable to fraternise with the punters outside the club. What you see isn't always what you get. Both ways.'

'Yes, well, I know that now,' said Tina. 'Honestly, if I could turn back the clock ...'

A big man in a black crombie barged past her and ran out of the café. Started yelling at the drunken Santa Clause.

'Excuse me would be nice,' said Tina. She looked down and saw that she'd spilled her coffee over the table cloth. Picked up a couple of napkins to wipe it up.

'Still, you could have had worse,' said Ania. 'Him, for example.' She sipped her green tea as she watched the fat man start jabbing Santa in the chest, causing Father Christmas to puke.

Tina chuckled to herself. Eyes twinkling.

'Yeah, at least Sebastian is in decent nick for his age. Hung like a donkey, too. But I thought being a rock star's totty would be a tad more exciting than this.'

'Former rock star, kochanie,' purred Ania. 'Former. That is the operative word. It's been years since his band had a hit. Though someone told me they could be due for a revival.'

'Like Dracula,' said Tina. She winced as Santa Clause head-butted the man in the Crombie, causing him to stagger.

Ania patted Tina's hand.

'Let's be honest. It's better than working in the club or going back to pickpocketing tourists, eh? Take it step by step. It'll get easier,' said Ania.

Tina knew that she was right. Ania was only a few years older than her, in her early thirties but she had been working as a high class escort for over a decade. Acted as if she'd seen it all and probably had. She was, Tina realised, the closest thing to a friend that she had though she really wouldn't trust Ania as far as she could throw her. She was sure the feeling was mutual.

'I couldn't go back to the club, though,' said Tina.

'I doubt Boris would let you, darling. He was very hurt when you left. Sebastian was one of his best cash-cows.'

Tina finished her coffee.

'I need something stronger. Up for a bit of a boozing session?'

'I really would, darling,' said Ania. 'But I've a full night of flogging ahead of me.'

Outside, Santa pushed the fat businessman against the window, which shattered, showering the café with broken glass. Ania got to her feet quickly, knocking over the contents of the table behind her. The café was a cacophony of screams and wails. The barista rushed toward the fat man.

'Are you okay, kochania,' said Ania. She plucked a tiny shard of glass from her cheek.

'Yes, I'm fine. In a better state than him anyway,' she nodded toward the fat businessman. He was flat on his back, red faced. Someone was giving him CPR.

'Let's get out of here,' said Ania. 'I can't be bothered with a long drawn out police interview.'

They both collected their belongings. As she picked up her chair, Tina noticed a small, oval shaped parcel on the floor. Pink wrapping paper and a polka-dot bow. She looked around but no one was watching her. Quick as a flash, she slipped it in her jacket pocket. As they stepped out onto the high street, snow fell like confetti.

'Want to share a cab?' said Tina. She put up a black umbrella.

'You don't live near my way,' said Ania. Turned up the collar of her overcoat.

'I'm not going home, am I? Home's where you go when you've nowhere better to go to.'

An ambulance pulled up as they crossed to road to the taxi rank.

'The Black Jack?' said Ania.

'Why not?' said Tina. 'It'll kill time as much as anything.'

'Why kill time when …'

'When I can kill Sebastian?' said Tina. They both burst out laughing.

†††

'I'm so pissed off,' said Sarah Malone. 'I really am. I'm super pissed off.'

She marched up and down in the hospital carpark puffing on a menthol cigarette, her long blonde hair glowing in the wind.

'I thought you wanted the fat twat dead? Out of the way?' said Catherine, dumpy and dowdy, nothing like her older sister.

'Yeah, of course I did, sis. He's well past his sell-by- date, you know that. But I wanted it done my way. Without questions. If he croaks now, someone might have a nosy into the insurance contracts. And then I'm fucked.'

'What do the quacks say?'

'Exhaustion, would you believe. That and boozing and pill popping in the morning.'

'So, he's going to be alright?'

'Yeah, that's not the point, though. The daft bastard has lost the ring.'

'The Himmler ring? Didn't know he'd found it,' said Catherine. She popped a Trebor mint into her mouth.

'Yeah, took him long enough but he got it. Even told Wally. And now, as luck would have it, he's lost it again.'

'Wally will not be pleased,' said Catherine.

An ambulance skidded into the car park, narrowly missing Sarah and Catherine.

†††

The band in The Black Jack really were bloody torture. A bunch of saggy BOFs. Some painful, horrible hybrid of blues rock and folk rock. Even the few songs that Tina recognised were mangled into some sort of plodding anonymity. Whisky in the Jar. Born to Run. Brass in Pocket. They all sounded the bloody same. The singer wasn't bad but he seemed to fancy himself as Jim Morrison and he really was far too old for those leather trousers.

And there was no talent in the place at all. Just a bunch of sweaty middle aged men in supermarket jeans. The singer started moaning about how, if it wasn't for bad luck he'd have no luck at all. Tell me about it.

She sighed and opened up the box she found in the cafe. Took out the ring. Held it up to the light. Grimaced

'A very tasty Totenkopfring, that. I used to have one of them,' said a fat biker who with a pin-size roll up stuck to his bottom lip.'

'Yeah,' said Tina 'What's one of them when it's at home?'

'An honour ring. Sometimes known as a death's head ring. Himmler dished them out to the SS, back in the day. Bloke over Camden used to knock them out.'

'Worth much?' said Tina. She wondered if it was antique. Maybe she could sell it to a collector. Get the fuck out of dodge.

'Naw, they're ten a penny. If it was an original, yes but no chance of that.'

Tina finished her drink. Slid the ring over to the biker.

'There you go mate,' she said.

She got up and put on her coat, collected her bag.

'Ta much!' said the biker. 'Here, darlin', any chance of a shag as well?'

He winked.

'You should be so lucky,' said Tina.

As she stepped outside, it started to rain.

Paul D. Brazill *is the author of A Case Of Noir, Guns Of Brixton, Cold London Blues, and The Gumshoe, and Other Brit Grit Yarns. He was born in England and lives in Poland. He is an International Thriller Writers Inc member whose writing has been translated into Italian, Finnish, German and Slovene. He has had writing published in various magazines and anthologies, including The Mammoth Books of Best British Crime. He has edited a few anthologies, including the best-selling True Brit Grit – with Luca Veste*

The Moon Tonight

Steve Weddle

This happened late one August when I was staying with some family around Calhoun.

Richelle had taken Landon and gone to stay with her mother for a while. I don't even remember what it was about that time, but a few days alone in the house seemed like a good idea. I could get up when I wanted, spend as long in the workroom as I wanted, finish a few things I'd started a while back. This was a couple months after the tire place had let me go, and back when anything was still possible.

I was talking to Bethany at the bonfire they used to keep running just south of Smackover where that all-you-can-eat seafood place used to be.

"She's three now," Bethany said, staring off at the moon, soft-edged and blurred with distance. Bethany and I had fooled around in high school and the years since hadn't been as bad to her as they had been to most of the others.

"What's her name, again?" She'd said the kid's name a few times in the story already. Something about how she started reading at 20 months because they'd done the whole nursery in red and white and black, like they'd read about in a magazine in the doctor's office before they lost their insurance.

"You see, red's the power, the fire color," she said, being someone who's read about fire but never seen it up close. Never felt it reaching for you, the pores on your forearms turning to pinkish welts, clear, wet welts as you hold your forearm against a campfire to prove you can still feel something. The hair all over you, curling back, soot-tipped, into your skin. Someone who does a thing, who makes a change because of what she's read in somebody else's office, what's she's heard other people say. "And black and white, why, that's the balance in nature." She said "ying and yang" like she was naming twins from a 70's cartoon.

"Flora," she said. "Her name's Flora."

I nodded, said the kid's name again, as if this time it would stick, as if it even mattered at that point to anyone but her and family services.

"So you never said what brought you down here. You still married? Someone online, Terry McWaters, you probably don't remember him, from over to Ware, he said you were married and working up around Chicago or St. Louis or somewhere? He's up at the new plant now."

"My uncle's funeral is tomorrow." It wasn't why I was there, but I didn't see the point in getting into everything with her at that point. Her husband would be off work soon.

She said oh, she was sorry to hear that.

"One of the last from the big war living around here."

She asked which one that was.

"World War Two. He served in the Pacific," I said. "Battle of Saipan."

She said was that China.

"Japan. Five grand jumped off a cliff instead of being captured."

She took a quick gulp from her can of beer, asked if it was us or them that jumped.

I said it was the Japanese.

She said that was a shame. Said they could have had a good life in America. "You remember Becky Thurman? She married a Japanese. I think he's a deacon now." She couldn't remember what church.

I bent my empty can, set it under my chair, reached for hers and drank what was left. I said I had an ice chest in my car and most of a carton of cigarettes. She wrote a phone number on a napkin, but she wasn't interested in anything I was offering right then. And, I guess, I wasn't interested in offering her anything she'd want.

At the service the next day, another of my uncles, the youngest of the brothers, said a few words, mostly thanking everyone for coming. He didn't say anything about the Pacific Theater, which my uncle used to talk about and for years I'd thought was a movie house in Hawaii. He didn't talk about the scars, the ink my uncle showed everyone. He didn't talk about the purpose my uncle had had in the war, the stories he told as he drifted from jobs at a dairy farm, a light bulb factory, the paper mill, the Walmart. He said my uncle was a good man who had lived a good life and had gone to his great reward in the sky.

The funeral home was separated from the highway by a two-row parking lot and sporadic boxwoods. We were in the larger of the two chapel rooms, the Atrium of Comfort. Across the hall and past the restrooms, in the Atrium of Peace, family and friends crying over the closed casket of a woman who, going by the picture on the bulletin wall directing traffic, was a glowing beauty back before talkies.

The remains of my uncle were to be scattered along some family land they owned at Glaze Creek where they'd been burying their pets for decades. A man in uniform played "Taps," as everyone stared motionless at the walls. Another man, someone's minister, said he'd like to say a few words and then did.

I was standing at the back of the mostly empty room when the man from the American Legion tried handing the flag to my cousin.

"What's that?"

"My condolences on the loss of your father, Mr. Rainey."

"Alright," he nodded, looked away.

The man held the flag out, triangle-folded and crisp. The man from the American Legion kept his eyes towards my cousin without really looking at him, the way you might look at but not focus on your wife when she kept talking about what someone on TV had said to someone else on TV or what she thought you should have told the marriage counsellor instead of what you'd said.

I'd had to borrow a jacket from one of the hall closets in my cousin's house. One of the outside pockets had moth-balls, the other pocket had cough drops. Inside was a folded card for someone else's funeral a couple years back. When

Richelle and I started dating, her father would answer the
door. He'd always ask if he could take my jacket, even though
I wasn't wearing one. Every time I'd tell him no thanks and
every time he'd say "Maybe next time," like he was trying
to prove a point. Last August someone shot him outside a
Brookshire's for no real reason.

"What's that?" my cousin asked again.

"Staff Sergeant Rainey's flag."

My cousin looked at me. His top lip was up and his eye-
brows down in the "do you believe this shit?" look he used
sometimes when we would come across people at gas stations
or malls.

"He wants to give you your father's flag. From the cere-
mony," I said, then tried smiling at the flag man.

"Tell him I don't want the goddamn flag," he said.

The flag man looked to me.

"Tell him I'm a pacifist," my cousin explained.

"It's your dad's flag. Just take it," I said, leaning closer to
him. When my cousin folded his arms, I turned to the flag
man, thanked him, said it was nice of them all to go to the
trouble for the family, and took the flag.

The man from the American Legion nodded, snapped his
shoes like a crease, then went away.

"You didn't have to be a dick about it," I said.

"You have any idea what Reagan did in Central America?
People just forget about that. People don't stand up for any-
thing. Ever hear of Halliburton? What the Bushes did in
Kurdistan?"

I said no, not really, I guess.

"You knew half, hell, no, you knew one percent of what

they've done behind that flag, you wouldn't be holding it, either. Damn corporate oligarchy, man. That's all that flag is. You wouldn't be sitting here and taking in all this bullshit, all these toy soldiers. They're the dicks, man, not me. I didn't do anything. Just ask them. Blood ain't on my hands."

I said they were just wanting to honor his father.

"My father's dead. It doesn't matter now."

†††

After I'd handed the flag to one of my other uncles, I stepped outside for a smoke, dialed Richelle's number to check on Landon. Didn't leave a message at the beep.

I held the ashed embers of the cigarette up against the moon, the darkening flakes like loosed craters in shadows, the flame rim of the paper an imperfect ridge against the moon's edge, carving in and out in no real pattern. Just jagged pieces falling apart, drifting nowhere slowly.

The flag man was talking on his cell phone at the corner of the building. When he was done, I walked towards him, said it was a nice night out.

He said it was.

"Don't worry about my cousin," I said. "Just having a tough time. You know, the funeral."

"Families, am I right?"

I said he was right.

He said he'd seen all kinds, said funerals can get to people, even the best of people.

I said, "So many of these World War Two soldiers dying these days." After Richelle had taken Landon and before I'd decided what to do, I'd read an article about dying soldiers in a magazine she'd left on the kitchen table. Or seen something on the TV. Or neither.

He said, "Yeah."

"Hundreds a day."

"Not around here," he said.

"No. Not around here, I guess. Must get to you after a while."

"Well, I don't know most of them. They're all pretty old."

"I just mean going to the funerals and services and all the families. Must get to you."

"Just part of my service to my country," he said, like he was reading off a pamphlet.

"Right. Still, all that loss. Somber. People getting choked up. You must get tired of playing it," I said, not being able to imagine it. The respect, the honor. Standing there with the families, saying the right thing, following exactly what they're supposed to be doing. "I mean, maybe you guys get used to it, but doing that, I mean, that's solid," I said, though it wasn't exactly the word I meant.

"Part of the job," he said.

I said, "But still." The pressure. All that loss. Everything right on the edge of leaving, of falling apart. Everything worth anything too far away, too many good things in the past you'll never have again, too many things out of reach. Stuck in the now, where nothing is worth dreaming about, worth reaching for. All the things within reach, realizing one night back from the counsellor, one clear night. I looked from the moon to the man. I said at least he was bringing comfort, a memory of being a soldier. I said he was leaving the family with an image of a soldier, an image of someone who fought for us all. Someone who believed in a thing and could have died for it. No matter what, I told him, at least there was that and he was giving them that. I said I didn't know how he did it, funeral after funeral, standing there and giving that to the families, giving them something real they could hold.

He reached down, picked the bugle up off the bench. He held up the horn, the street lights of the parking lot shooting little stars from the horn's edge. He let the light catch inside the bell-end. "See that," he said, showing me a small plastic box inside. "It's a little music player. I just hit this button and it plays the song for me. I just have to stand up here and hold the horn to my face like I'm playing and close my eyes until the song's over."

"It plays 'Taps' for you?"

He said it did. Said it played up to 30 songs, if you wanted.

I didn't know what to say. "What else does it play?" I was thinking of bugle songs I knew. The boogie woogie one the Andrew Sisters sang in the old movies. Something I could remember. Something I'd seen.

"Nothing else. Never needed anything but 'Taps,'" he said.

†††

I drove down to Calion Lake after the funeral. Arnie Baker and I had found some Koroan arrowheads back when we were kids, down there along Yellow Bluff. His sister had been dating a graduate student from Little Rock who was working on De Soto's trip through Arkansas, and he'd given us each ten bucks for them. The people living in Arnie's house had pulled up all the shrubs, replaced the siding with bricks, and paved the driveway with purpose, with certainty. The tree we'd climbed up to shoot pellet guns at passing trucks was even gone. Or maybe I was looking at the wrong house.

I parked at an auto store, took a warm six-pack from the backseat, walked around the town until I found a cemetery I could sit in and watch the lake. I hung the last two cans of beer I had left from chain link fence I was leaning against, and waited for the moon to come over the lake. It was just at a point in the sky where it wouldn't reflect off the water, even when I leaned my head all the way against the ground in front of one of the headstones, name worn illegible.

Thirty years back, more or less, Arnie Wascom and I had gone into the woods, followed a fence to breaking where we found a sort of clearing. I was staying with my uncle that summer while my folks worked through the divorce. Arnie's father was a family doctor, had moved them from somewhere in the northeast, two German cars and a liquor cabinet against a small town of ice chest beer and gravel, a small town where the retired surgeon had set the legs of three dogs in a year, where the vet had paid for his lakehouse with a horse tranq ring at the high school.

Arnie had an army surplus shovel and wax-dipped matches from a scout catalog, and when we got to the fence break, we peeled the barbed wire back until it rust-snapped apart, shards of nail that had once held a thing together. We twisted tight lines of thin pines, sharpened and leaned against one another, a rampart wall against Nazis, Indians, the weather. Underneath us, a hardpacked floor, pineneedles swept clear with a pineneedle broom.

I'd brought down a busted .22 bolt-action rifle from my

uncle's house. Arnie had a pellet gun and a knife with waxed matches, hooked fishing line, and a piece of flint in the handle. We stalked shuffling sounds through the softened edges of late morning until we found a nest of dead squirrels in the heart of a tree. I took the biggest baby, still warm, into the inside pocket of my jacket until, summer heat and pressure, he started melting against my side, sliding damp, tacky along my ribs. Arnie knife-tipped the others in the eyes.

On the way back to my uncle's, I hand-dug a divot into the earth, laid down what was left of the squirrel among broken stones, imaginary arrowheads. Before I was clear of the treeline, he was already giving in to the clay around him.

I took the two cans from the fence near me, knifed a hole into the base of the first, shotgunned the warmth, the bitter thinness, tossed the can against the headstone of some asshole I'd never heard of. I made a pillow of the funeral jacket, pulled my phone from my pocket as I watched the moon move in and out of clouds. I hummed the first three notes of "Taps," raised the pitch as I went along in the song until I got lost, looking out under the moonlit haze, past the suits and dress shoes fading to dust and ash underneath me, past the arrowheads and squirrels, past spotlit flags and chests of medals. I slid the phone back in my pocket and walked towards home.

Steve Weddle *teaches writing for LitReactor, blogs at DoSomeDamage, and edits Needle: A Magazine of Noir.*
His debut novel, Country Hardball, is published in North America by Tyrus Books. His website is www.steveweddle.com.

Hod County

Court Merrigan

We was traversing a two-lane highway down across the green hills. I was in a car of foreign make, a 1977 Mazda, and so was Hawk, a 1981 Datsun pickup truck, yellow. Up and down those green hills along a two-lane highway and the going was slow, for this was Mennonite country. Many folks held to the old ways of an old country, to include horse-and-buggy contraptions that did gum up the traffic to a crawl. They seemed right sullen about it, too, hunched on their seats as if they expected to be cursed at, and they was, by me, from behind my windshield, ranting and raving and generally carrying on about how they was dangerously holding up progress. But I never honked at a one. Hawk, he did, though. He laid on the horn a time or two, and I resolved that at our next stopping point I would speak to him, because such behavior seemed to me inexcusably rude and anyway the plan called for us to pass through this country multiple times on our runs. It wouldn't do to go making enemies of the local folk the very first time through.

I remember one fellow in particular looked in particular grim. Massive man, his buggy tilted clear to his side on its axles. He must of weighed three-fifty in overalls. Snapping reins upon the horse's back something furious like he was after something and those poor creatures straining best they could up the hill, a right smart trot, which still didn't amount to fifteen miles per, which is no kind of pace to get somewhere, in my judgment. But my judgment and that of a man who'll insist upon a horse and buggy in this year of our Lord are not to be considered of a kind, and when the highway cleared, me and Hawk both passed him and I saw in the rearview how he never looked anywhere but ahead, Abe Lincoln beard with the bare upper lip and the chin and jaw engulfed in chestnut whiskers, angry at the world or at least some members thereof.

Soon thereafter I was possessed of nature's urgings too fierce to deny them further, so I pulled over at a stretch clear of horse-drawn contraptions and cars but, as I am of a modest nature, I did betake myself into the trees to attend to my business while Hawk rolled on ahead. I figured I would catch up to him sure enough at the next bend in the highway where traffic was waylaid by a horse and buggy. It was pretty country, too, and after concluding my business in the trees I leaned against the ticking hot hood of that Mazda to admire the neat white Mennonite barns and the rows in the fields laid out just so. They'd made it into a pretty country, the Mennonites hereabouts, that credit you must extend them. Then I climbed back in the cab and commenced onwards.

It was near upwards of ten more miles before I caught up to Hawk and when I did there were two items to notice about that yellow Datsun: it was running a flat on the front passenger side and on the passenger side was seated a passenger.

Hawk had shown himself in the past to be not averse to companionship along the road but it seemed this companion was more distracting than most, for if he'd gained awareness of his flat-rolling tire, he gave no sign. We got ourselves around another horse-and-buggy and then on a flat stretch where I could see a mile or more ahead, I pulled alongside the Datsun, got Hawk's attention and pointed out the problem on his passenger side.

Hawk, he was grinning to beat the devil and he nodded along in the throes of enthusiasm which I inferred to plainly refer to his passenger. Who, upon the glance I was able to give her before pulling ahead of Hawk owing to an oncoming automobile, was a Mennonite girl.

Like I say, Hawk, he was given to companionship and this was not the first companion of the female variety he had happened upon the road. Afterwards he was always full of big stories about what all it could have been like if she had been a titch more friendly, but for reasons all their own he'd yet to share cab space and road miles with a woman hitchhiker who was as amorously friendly as he'd of liked. In any case, he was bound to take this passenger just about anywhere she desired, being a gentleman. Besides, she wore the Mennonite bonnet and the long Mennonite sleeves so her destination couldn't be far, given how folks of her horse-drawn ilk draw themselves shorter horizons than them of us who take to the road in motorized transport. Therefore I waved out the window to Hawk and ventured on. He was going to have to change that tire himself. Maybe he could get his passenger to help him out.

I did not make more than twenty or twenty-five miles

down that two-lane blacktop, though, before I was wracked by doubt and stricken by conscience. The doubt proceeding from my deep uncertainty that that Datsun when we acquired it had a spare tire, the conscience proceeding from my having left behind Hawk in a fit of pique, Hawk, my brother of the road. A third consideration, too, was that our funds was at something of a low ebb, this trip being undertaken for the express purpose of replenishing them. There was therefore little in the way of funds for a new tire. We could, however, convey the tire we did possess and leave the Datsun sit roadside while I piloted the Mazda to a repair shop. I had seen just such an establishment in the town through which I'd lately passed. I'd be gracious, too, and take along Hawk's passenger that far. She could sit in the middle. It would be of great interest to be in such close proximity to a Mennonite girl and this a narrow front seat, the back seat being presently missing from the vehicle. My jeans was threadbare and I thought, I confess, that I might even be able to get the feel of her dress. It is nothing as exciting as a woman covered up every inch of her, that you know you never can have.

I passed back through that town, name of Falls City, and then some miles back beyond, and did not encounter that Datsun. I wondered if Hawk had not arranged for a tow but reasoned it could not of happened so quickly, nor would Hawk have been so profligate with our dwindling funds. So I turned round and drove more slowly this time, peeking into the barnyards of the farmhouses behind their neat Mennonite tree rows as I passed, thinking Hawk, he might of pulled into one, seeking assistance, though what assistance folks who will use horses and buggies in this day and age would be prepared to render, I could in no way infer. No Hawk though, and no Datsun. It occurred to me that the girl had asked for a lift some ways off the main highway and if so, I faced rapid dwindling odds of locating him. The plan was we was to stick together all the way but then I had forsaken that plan, had I not?-and Hawk may have felt himself justified in straying from the agreed-upon route himself.

I cursed myself and slammed the heels of my hands into the steering wheel but this did not locate Hawk nor the yellow Datsun and so I drove back through the town, name of Falls City. Turned off onto a side street and pulled into the gravel lot of an abandoned gas station so as to ponder the next move without wasting further fuel. I could envision Hawk pulling into the grateful barnyard of a family missing their daughter and lacking even a telephone to ask the neighbors or authorities if they had seen her and Hawk, gregarious and accepting of gratitude, sitting to a meal with them, that Mennonite girl serving him milk shyly out of a pitcher. And the father insisting they assist this man who'd returned their daughter, and so the tire loaded up in the buggy, and off to town to find a tire mechanic, a journey which would consume an entire day. Twould make a right good story, all right, and it would all begin with how I roared off and left him in a huff.

I was further mulling upon this plotline when I glimpsed through the side window the edge of a back pickup truck bumper that looked almighty familiar.

"Hawk?" I said, aloud, being so thoroughly consternated by this juncture that I was speaking to myself.

I engaged the Mazda and pulled around the corner of the abandoned gas station to discover a tumbledown motel, a line of half a dozen rooms fronting a further weedy lot and a cracked and crumbling side road, still in operation. The Datsun one of two automobiles pulled up to the motel, paint peeling and plaster cracking and windows dirty, the other being a long purple Pontiac pulled up in front of the Office. The yellow Datsun rested at the odd angle of an upward slope and a now entirely flat front passenger tire and it sat empty, parked before Room #3.

I killed the Mazda next to the Datsun, unbelieving at this turn of events. Upon searching my memory and it'd indeed been a Mennonite girl riding shotgun, none but one so faithful would of garbed herself so, and so what was the Datsun doing at this cheap motel?

I did slam the Mazda door hard, hoping to attract attention from inside Room #3, but no such luck, even after I waited. So I went to the door and knocked. There emanated a sound like a body as it would fall perpendicular from a bed and then a heavy tread to the door, which opened a crack, and there was a slice of Hawk's face.

"Shit, Cy," Hawk said, a further glance revealing that Hawk had arrived door side in the altogether, "you scared hell out of me."

"What are you doing?" I said in plain bewilderment.

"Who's that, Hawk?"

A female voice, from inside the room. I knew instantly though I could not all the way bring myself to believe that it was the Mennonite girl.

"Friend of mine," Hawk said.

"Well, don't be rude," the voice said.

Hawk grinned at me sheepishly. "She will have her ways,"

he said.

He closed the door and slid loose the chain and then re-opened the door wide, holding a pillow over his modesty, gesturing emperor-like for me to enter. Which I did. And there was that Mennonite girl, Mennonite garb scattered around the slight furnishings of the narrow room, in the bed, a solitary sheet only modestly covering her modesty.

"Cy," Hawk said, "meet Ludmila."

"How do?" Ludmila said, extending a hand, and so dropping what remained of her modesty. Hawk shut the door behind me.

Yes, Ludmila may have been a Mennonite girl bearing an old name of an old country but she was fairly bursting with what I suppose you might call modern energy. She said when she saw Hawk pull over on that road to pick her up she knew everything about her life was about to change though from her ministrations in the bed and upon the floor and in the cracked green bathtub, I had a hard time believing this was her maiden journey into the ways of all flesh but as with Hawk, similarly taken, I did not care.

She took us one at a time, she took us both at a time, she utilized the room phone to call a friend of hers at a public phone who arrived not an hour later and proved to be just as lusty as Ludmila herself, though she did not consent to stay the night, and I never did learn her name.

We was awakened midmorning next morning by the inn-keep, demanding another day's lodging as we had overstayed check-out time by more than half an hour. Like I say, our funds was precious but Ludmila was grinning from the bed so I doled out the amount the innkeep demanded, and thence we was left alone. We sported the rest of that morning and by midday we'd taken to swapping spit for sustenance, Ludmila crowing that she had a lot more nutrition in her than us two.

"I am plain tapped out, honey," Hawk said. "I got no more to give."

"Me either," I said.

"Let's go eat then," Ludmila said. "My friend you met yesterday, she works sometimes at the joint down the street."

"I thought you Mennonites wasn't allowed to work off the farm," Hawk said.

Ludmila shrugged. "Her father drinks."

"How about your father?" I asked.

"Oh, no," Ludmila said. "He is faithful to the old ways."

In the joint, name of Waysider Cafe, divesting ourselves of more of the funds growing more precious by the hour in exchange for flapjacks and steak and black coffee, we learned that we was in a county name of Hod. We learned this from the Sheriff of Hod County, who was, as he said, enjoying himself a cup of coffee before returning to his duties maintaining peace and good order in said Hod County, which personal peace and good order he could not enjoy his own self, seeing the general ruckus the three of us was making at our table, all three of us crammed together in one side of the bench, Ludmila twixt Hawk and me.

"We are sorry, officer," Hawk said.

Ludmila choked back a giggle, whereupon I could hardly restrain myself and Hawk, he spit up coffee right upon the Sheriff's shoes.

The Sheriff of Hod County, he didn't move, though. He acted like he'd seen all this before.

"I never forget a face," he said, and then his radio squawked. He tipped his hat to the waitress throwing us dirty looks like to melt a stone gargoyle from the counter.

We didn't worry none about the Sheriff of Hod County. I didn't figure even in Mennonite country you could get arrested for giggling in a coffee shop. I did, however, in good conscience, tip that scowling waitress the full amount of the bill, never mind the damage done to the precious funds. I believe in making things right where I can, and running fast where I can't.

It was another day and night of fun after that. Ludmila informed us she was freshly seventeen years old. By God, she had the energy of three women, and I was plain tuckered out and sore next morning just after break of dawn, waking to push Hawk's arm off my chest where he'd flopped it seeking Ludmila, who was out of bed, near full dressed.

"I got to go home," she said.

I slipped out of bed, thinking for one more go-around, thinking it'd be fun to see her going at it with her clothes on but she slapped my seeking hand away.

"I got to go home," she said again.

"All right," I said. "Where's home?"

"Get yourself dressed," Ludmila said. "You, too," she said to Cy, looking up bleary-eyed from the pillow. "I'll sit twixt you and show you the way."

Precious funds or no I could of used a cup of coffee before setting out but Ludmila was adamant we get a move on, all folded up neat in her Mennonite skirt and her Mennonite bonnet, hands folded prim upon her lap except when they was slapping one or the other of our straying hands away.

She had turned herself complete into another person, of the faithful old type, for reasons she chose not to reveal, which transmogrification I could respect, and halfway to her place I was already thinking of getting on down the road, and how me and Hawk would manage now that we'd blown our budget all to hell and gone.

I did get to feel the feel of a Mennonite skirt through my threadbare jeans, however. Tingly.

Ludmila's home was far out upon an interminable set of blacktop and gravel roads, another neat white Mennonite home, with a neat white barn and horses poking their heads from the stalls. A neat white curl of smoke from the chimney. Even the white chickens looked clean. Ludmila climbed out of the Mazda and the three of us approached the door. Ludmila, being of the house, did not knock, but slipped right on in. Hawk and me weren't sure whether to follow, Ludmila having not said so much as goodbye, but our decision was made for us in the next moment when that doorway was filled up in its entirety by an enormous man in Mennonite overalls with an enormous chest-length Abe Lincoln beard and bare upper lip. I'd seen the man just two days prior, slapping the reins merciless upon the rumps of his team.

"You are the two, then," he said, voice a fair roar.

"I guess so, sir," I said.

"We just wanted to give her a ride, sir," Hawk said. "We didn't mean to have her home so late."

"Didn't mean to?!!?" roared Ludmila's father.

"Well, sir, we kindly got caught up in a matter or two," Hawk said.

"Disgrace and wrack and ruin brought upon my house by

my slattern of a daughter!" Ludmila's father roared. "And here before me stand the instruments of her downfall!"

"We didn't mean to cause nothing in the way of wrack and ruin, sir," I said.

"We'll just be going," Hawk said, taking a step back.

"One of you will be going!" Ludmila's father yelled. "On to hell, and that is certain. The other of you, you will redeem this sin."

Me and Hawk eyed one another because we took his meaning, all right, but didn't either of us quite believe it. Hawk took him another step back.

"One of you will stay!" bellowed Ludmila's father, and through a tiny shifting gap between his bulk and the doorframe I saw Ludmila, cowering, and I hesitated, when I should of been doing what Hawk was doing. Running. But: "You then!" Ludmila's father bellowed. The giant of a man pointed at me with a bony finger stiff with black hair and I could not but obey. Behind me slammed the door and outside the Mazda engine roared to life.

Well, sir: you may not believe such events do occur in this day and age and in this country, but you were not the one on his knees, fingers laced through the fingers of his now-betrothed, father of your betrothed wielding a great leather strap with which, he bellowed again, he would suck the sin from your bodies as Zophar the Naamathite of the Bible sucked forth the venom of the snake, yea, the selfsame snake as ensnared foolish woman Eve into sin at the beginning of time. He wielded that leather strap with consummate skill and Ludmila, who'd felt its bite before, did bear up better under the scourge than I, who was begging for mercy inside of three licks. Ludmila had a little sister, in long Mennonite frock, summoned to watch our chastisement as warning and precaution against her own sinful and devious female nature, made to stand right beside us on our knees, and Ludmila's father did not cease until her face was flecked with blood spattered from my back.

Hawk, meanwhile, coasted into the town of Falls City upon fumes and found the Sheriff of Hod County in the Waysider Cafe, draining the dregs of a coffee cup.

"Please," Hawk said.

The Sheriff of Hod Country looked him over. "I never forget a face," he said, and held up a hand to stifle Hawk's objections. "And you got the face of a man who isn't given to an understanding of how things work here in Hod County. Do you suggest I intrude upon the doings of a man in his own private domicile?"

"But he has Cy, like I was telling you!" Hawk said.

"This Cy entered into that house upon his own free will, did he not?"

"Sure, but ..."

Again the Sheriff of Hod County held up a hand to silence Hawk's talk. "This county is filled with miscreants and evildoers. Isaac Stoltzfus isn't among them. I'm not about to drive out to his place on the suspicious talk of some outsider yokel who spit upon my boots no more long ago than yesterday. Now, if you were at all wise, you would be taking yourself down upon the road to wherever it is you were headed when you entered my fair county to begin with. Lest you find yourself classified amongst the miscreants and the evildoers. You take my meaning, hoss?"

Hawk did. Which was why I did not see him among the well-wishers three days later when I stood before a Mennonite preacher, rough-sewn Mennonite shirt sticky upon my oozing back, arm interlocked with Ludmila's, blushing not from the bashfulness of bridedom but from the effort required to keep herself from crying out as her simple Mennonite wedding frock did rub against her same raw wounds, to which her father had returned with bellowing enthusiasm each of these past three days gaining our consent to the nuptials he planned. Binding for all eternity, he said, such as to save your wretched souls.

Court Merrigan lives in Wyoming. He's the author of Moondog Over The Mekong and short stories all over. He's currently at work on a novel.

More at @courtmerrigan

Trash

Todd Robinson

Twenty-five tons of garbage truck made a sharp left onto Mott St. Will stood on the back runner, his fingers laced through the railing. The summertime stink of Chinatown started polluting his sinuses from three blocks away. These blocks were the worst of the run, the smell of rotting seafood was one that wouldn't leave his nose for a few hours. It roosted inside his nasal cavity like an Alphabet City squatter.

It was worse that Will could have imagined. Even worse that the detailed descriptions his old man had given him about the bad old days.

The elder Mr. Pokorski had warned Will long before he'd set his son up with the job for the summer. The trash route Will was on was the same that his father had done up until his retirement three years ago. It was a soft scam going back generations. A lot of Union guys, especially the ones who worked the roughest summer runs, would pay the sons of other Union members ten bucks an hour and pocket the rest of their salary for the additional days off. Some guys, like the one Will was covering, were willing to sacrifice the money for the entire summer so long as it meant they wouldn't have to deal with Chinatown at all for the season.

Will absolutely understood the reasons now.

Even though the sun had set a full five hours ago, the heat that had been absorbed deeply into the concrete radiated up in waves, cooking the filth like a convection oven. What sat at the bottom of the black garbage bags was now slow-cooking from the ground up.

Like he tended to do, Antoine made the left hard and fast, disregarding the fact that the light had turned full red a good three seconds before he accelerated into the turn. Two cars let loose with a horn blare as they screeched to short stops.

Will was trying to keep the fetid air at bay by keeping his nose and mouth covered with the crook of his elbow as they sped down the street. When Antoine made another attempted Tokyo Drift move with the garbage truck, the centrifugal force nearly tore Will off the back. "Slow down, you freakin' lunatic!"

Antoine haw-hawed his ass off in the drivers' seat. Will could see his fat frame bouncing up and down in laughter through the big side mirror. Just the day before, a hard turn onto Canal nearly turned a middle-aged woman's labradoodle into slurry under the truck's thick wheels.

When he started the job at the beginning of June, Will asked Antoine what was up with the New York City garbage trucks' disregard for traffic laws and public safety in general.

"Fuck em," was all Antoine answered with.

Back in the day, Antoine was one of the summertime kids, just like Will. Antoine had done the route with his old man, now a lifer with the Sanitation Dept.

Will had no intention of being a lifer. Even though he was sorely jealous of his friends who'd all thrown in for a rental down the shore for the summer, Will wanted the money. When he started the Criminal Law program at Long Island University in the fall, he had no intention of doing so while commuting out of his parents' home. Will was getting his own place with his girlfriend Cara. His buddies would still be living in their tiny childhood bedrooms with their Eli Manning posters and high school track trophies. Will was going to finally have his own space to bang his girlfriend without the threat of either his mother coming in, or worse... Cara's dad, the NYPD sergeant.

It was this promise of carnal freedom that kept Will hanging onto his sanity, kept him from seething at the thought of missing what was probably the last hurrah for high school on the shore.

It'll be worth it. It's all going to be worth it, he told himself over and over, every night.

The truck pulled up in front of Lucky Star Restaurant, and Will hopped off. He moved double-time while in Chinatown, wanting to get the hell gone before his gag reflex kicked in. He hurled the trash bags as quickly as he could into the rear of the truck.

One night after grousing about the run at the one bar in Staten Island with a bouncer dumb enough to accept his shitty Times Square fake I.D., a customer asked him how bad could the smell be? He was a garbage man, after all.

"How bad can it be?" Will replied. "I'm a goddamn garbage man, and the smell makes me want to puke. Every goddamn time. That's how bad the smell is."

He'd tried to use a facemask for a while, but after a couple of breaths, it only felt like the stink was trapped underneath the thin sheet of cotton, pressed even closer to his face.

There was nothing he could do about it other than hope for short summer months or for something inside his olfactory system to finally give up and die.

Will grabbed the last bag off the pile, the plastic drooping sadly next to a mostly disassembled chest of drawers. On the upswing towards the compactor well, the bag caught on an exposed screw and burst open like a ripe cyst, viscous liquid splattering along the front of his jumpsuit.

"Fuck," Will yelped as the warm fluid soaked through his clothing and boots. He stepped back and felt it squishing wet inside his socks. He was about to reflexively put his hand over his mouth in order to suppress the gagging that he felt rising inside him before he realized that his gloves were covered in what looked like rotting calamari in gelatin.

By the time all of his senses could coordinate which aspect to be horrified at (the answer being: all of it), Will's vision swam.

On top of everything else, Will had to worry about fainting out of sheer disgust. Took him a moment-a terrible, terrible moment, but then he noticed that his vision wasn't in fact swimming. What were swimming, however, were the hundreds of maggots embedded in the fluid that was covering him.

He nearly screamed.

He almost did.

But it's really hard to scream when you're projectile vomiting all over the side of a garbage truck on Mott St.

All the way down Mott St...

All the way to Oliver St...

Back up Katherine St. to Henry St...

Antoine haw-hawed so hard at Will that he nearly threw up himself. On the corner of Market, Antoine had to jump out of the truck's cab, heaving and haw-ing so loudly that a middle-aged Chinese lady started yelling at him out her window.

Will didn't understand the Mandarin that the woman was shrieking, but it was pretty easily translated into the old classic of NYC sentiments.

Shut the fuck up.

Will found himself lagging on the bag tosses. All of his prior instincts and muscle memory from the job abandoned him as he was filled with a new caution that he'd never had on the job before. Only a couple more blocks after Antoine nearly lost his dinner, he was whining at Will to speed it up. They were already a half-hour behind from their usual mark, and at their current pace, they were only going to fall farther behind.

But despite all sense of self-preservation towards his senses, Will didn't want to have another bag pop open on him. As it was, he was already dreading his girlfriend's reaction when he got home. She already gave him shit for coming into the apartment smelling the way he did after a normal night on the job, with no exploding bags of Chinatown muck in the mix.

And for some reason, he kept thinking about the Hispanic lady at the cleaners, who always looked at him like he was the worst person on earth when he walked through the door of her laundromat. If she held him in distaste before, she was going to love the bag he was going to drop off that night.

He didn't know why he feared the woman's ire, but he did.

That said, he carefully eyeballed every bag for tell-tale rips, lighter areas of plastic where the bag may be stretched to a point of near-breakage. Nor was he cavalierly chucking the bags into the back, either. Each bag, he lifted carefully, in not daintily, as far away from his body as he could, then lobbed them in the back with no more velocity that one would underhand a waffle ball to a toddler.

"You're killin' me, Will," Antoine whined.

Then the loosest of thoughts flittered across Will's mind as the truck pulled up in front of the Lotus Blossom Massage Parlor. It wasn't just that there were more bags in front of the tiny storefront than usual, but straight-up; why would a massage parlor have so much garbage?

Lost in that thought, Will lifted the first bag, the weight striking, almost making him miss the two dime-sized holes in the bag.

"Whoa, shit!" Will yelled.

"What is it now?" Antoine said.

"Holes in the bag."

"You're fucking killing me."

"You're mistaking me for heart disease, you tubby fuck."

That shut Antoine up for a second. Then, "That was a little mean."

Will rolled his eyes and put the bag carefully back down onto the sidewalk so he could find a better purchase for his grip. Then as the bag flattened back out under its own weight, two purple lacquered fingernails poked out through the holes. Fingernails that were still attached to fingers.

"Oh fuck!" Will jumped back like he'd found a live raccoon in the bag.

"What is wrong with you?" Antoine said, with even more exasperation than he'd already had in his voice for the past hour.

"There...there's a hand in there."

"What?" Antoine hopped out of the cab. "No way. Just toss it in."

"We have to call the cops."

"No. No we don't." Even under the poor light of the streetlamps, Will could see the color draining out of Antoine's normally ruddy face.

Then Will made the observation that the bag was way too small to have a whole body in it. But then again, there were more bags than usual.

If Will had anything left inside, he might have thrown up again. But this time he might never stop. "Fuck that. I'm calling the cops."

"You can't call the cops, you dumb little shit. You're gonna fuck me with the union that you're even here. Then you'll fuck yourself, and your old man. Put the bags in the fucking truck."

Goddammit. Antoine wasn't wrong. Will shook his head. "Don't care. You can take off. I'll wait here until the cops come."

"And then what?"

"I don't know! This is the first time I've discovered a fucking body." Will dialed 911.

"Will...listen to me very carefully. Put...the bags...in the truck."

Will didn't like the sudden change in Antoine's voice. He looked up. Antoine wasn't looking at Will or the bags any more, he was staring a laser beam into the window of The Lotus Blossom Massage Parlor.

Will followed his stare.

911. What is your emergency?

Will looked at his phone.

"Hang up, Will." There was a tremble in Antoine's voice that gave Will a shiver.

Against his better instincts, Will disconnected from the call, then followed Antoine's gaze.

In the window stood an elderly Chinese man, smoking a thin cigarette. His expression was as warm as a marble statue, the only movement in the tableau being his smoke lifting on the breeze and the incessant tick-tock of a waving lucky cat statue on the sill.

"Will, no more fucking around now," Antoine said.

Will swallowed a sour lump. "I'm not just going to throw her in the back. She was a person. Let's just go. I'll call the cops later," he said in a harsh whisper.

Will looked back to the window. The old man hadn't so much as blinked. Then, he flicked his fingertips towards Will, a long ash falling off the end of his cigarette, urging Will to get on with it.

Will shook his head. "No," he said softly, nearly a croak. He tried to clear his throat, but it was only dryness in there. "No," he said, a little louder.

The old man pursed his lips and looked to his left, nodded.

"Oh fuck," Antoine said. "Who did he just nod to?"

"Let's just go," Will said, hopping back on the truck's runner.

Then, Will heard a series of locks disengaging behind the thick door of Lotus Blossom Massage.

"Fucking drive, Antoine!"

"Just toss the bags in! They seen us. They know who we are."

"They don't know who we…"

"Listen to me, kid. Just throw the bags in." Antoine's voice was calmer than it had been for the last five minutes. Deathly calm.

Click.

The sound came from everywhere and nowhere, the sound carrying on the city night air.

Antoine's face went ghost white. "What was that click?"

Will's skin turned icy. His old man had taught him enough about guns on the range in Staten Island for him to recognize the sound.

Will couldn't explain the sensation, but he suddenly felt like the back of his head had a target hanging off it.

"Fuck this noise," Antoine said, reaching for the door handle.

"I don't think we should move right now, Antoine."

Even though Antoine might not have recognized the sound of a bullet being chambered, he certainly understood the seriousness in Will's tone. He froze.

With the gentle jingling of a hung bell, the door to the massage parlor opened.

A woman of indeterminate age due to the long shadows under the neon emerged from the parlor. She was dressed in a white t-shirt and jeans cut off at the knees, but moved with a grace one would normally associate with someone in a ball gown.

She walked over to Will, a slight smile on her lips. Closer, and under the streetlights, Will made her out to be somewhere in her mid-forties, maybe older.

With a dancer's grace, she lifted the first bag, the one with the poke holes in it from the painted fingernails. She walked it over to the truck and dropped it in the compactor well.

Will was frozen. He felt like a mouse trapped in the glare of a cobra.

"Wasn't that simple?" the woman said, just a breath of an accent left in her English.

"You…you can't do this. That's a person," Will said, hating the tremor he heard in his own voice.

The woman tsk-tsked at him, like he was a child who simply didn't understand. "That is not true, young man. What's in these bags is not a person." She picked up a second bag, placed it next to the first. "Not any more. What's in these bags is an assortment of meat, bones. Nothing more."

"She…was."

"Was what? Was, was, was. Why do you even care, garbage man?"

Her question caught Will by surprise.

She stared at him, through him. She waited for his answer.

"I…I don't know," he finally said.

The woman picked up a second bag. Will noticed that her fingernails were painted the same color as those on the hand inside that first bag. "We called her Amy. It was the name she'd chosen for herself when she came to America. Did you know that many Chinese adopt western names when they come here?"

Will shook his head.

"It makes it easier for your kind to remember us, our given names being too exotic for your lazy minds and tongues." She picked up another bag, dropped it in the well with a wet plop. "After a while, we forget our real names. Who we were."

The woman tried picking up another larger bag, but its weight caught her. "Help me with this one, please," she said, her voice dripping with a poisonous honey.

Will could still feel the target on the back of his head. He reached down and grabbed the bag towards the bottom, ignoring the sensation that he was embracing part of a torso, that it was the softness of a breast under the fingers of his left hand.

The two of them tipped the bag over the lip of the truck where it joined the others.

"Thank you," the woman said. "Was that so hard?"

Will almost replied, but kept silent.

"Her real name was Chao-xing. Do you know what that means?"

Will shook his head.

"In Chinese, it means 'morning star.' Just like the ones we can't see in this city. Too much light pollution. We forget that they're up there, but they are. Just like our old names. I used to look up in the sky, wondering where the stars were. When I was a little girl, I wanted to be an astronomer. But after so many years, I forgot where they were supposed to be."

The woman gave a wave over the bags in the truck.

"Amy never forgot. She never forgot who she once was, that she wanted to be a dancer. She was going to be in the New York Ballet. She should have forgotten, but she couldn't. She cried a lot. Her crying was bad for business. She tried to leave.

She tried to forget, but tried to forget the wrong things-forget who she'd become…and who Amy owed debts to."

With a light flourish, the woman tossed the last two small bags into the truck.

"Why?" Will asked.

"Why what?"

"Why are you telling me all of this?"

The woman's smile beamed. "You said that the flesh in those bags was a person. You were not incorrect. Now you know who that person was. Now you tell me, the ending of the story being the same no matter what you knew about who Amy used to be, do you feel any better knowing?"

Will shook his head.

"Didn't think you would." The woman pulled the lever, activating the rear compactor. The bags crunched wetly, disappearing under the hydraulic press. After the machine completed its cycle, she wiped her hands on her jeans, then pulled a few bills out from a pocket sewn tightly to her side.

She walked over to Will and slid the money into his chest pocket, the paper crinkling. Her other hand brushed a caress against his hip. In his ear, she whispered, "Best massage in New York, if you're ever back in the Chinatown."

Without feeling their movement, the woman's fingers were suddenly in front of Will's face, the wallet from his back pocket wiggling between them. She stepped back, opened his wallet and took out his driver's license.

"Hmmm," she said. "Mr. William Pokorski. 4489 37th Avenue, Queens."

Will swallowed hard as her eyes studies his face intently. A suddenly warm smile spread across her face.

"You must be Lee's son," she said.

Her words hit Will like a gut punch. "How…how do you know my father's name?" He realized he'd taken her bait as the words fell out of his mouth.

As she walked to the storefront door, she tossed Will's wallet over her shoulder. Without looking back, she said, "Always nice to see you too, Mr. Gutierrez."

Will shot Antoine a look. "How does she know your name, Antoine?"

Antoine's lips were pursed tight. His eyes dropped and moved around the filthy street, looking anywhere but at Will.

"How the fuck does she know you and my dad, Antoine?"

Antoine silently climbed back into the truck and shut the door.

Will looked at Antoine's face, set like stone, reflecting back in the rearview.

Then, with numb fingers, Will pulled himself back onto the truck's runner.

"Young man!" the woman called to him before Antoine could put the truck into drive.

Despite his better instincts, Will looked back.

The woman was still smiling. "Do you remember what her Chinese name was?"

Will couldn't. His silence hung in the air like the humidity.

"Didn't think so." She waved as she closed the door, wiggling her purple fingernails at him.

Antoine and Will didn't speak again for the rest of their blessedly short route. When they pulled into the depot on Long Island, the sun was already up, the early heat soaking through Will's coveralls. The stink returned to his senses with a vengeance. Will hadn't even noticed the smell for the last hour of the shift.

Before walking into the garage, Will pulled out the money from his pocket.

Four hundred dollars.

He looked up. Antoine was staring at the bills with an odd expression. Will peeled two of the hundreds off the top and offered them to Antoine. Antoine didn't say no, didn't even shake his head. He just pulled his backpack out of the truck's cab and walked inside the garage.

Will looked at the bills in his hand.

Her name was Chao-xing.

Will crumpled the bills and tossed them in the back with the rest of the trash.

He hoped he would forget.

But he didn't.

TODD ROBINSON *writes stuff. Edits other stuff. He's got a book out and another one coming.*

Dispatch from Blue Skies

Les Edgerton

MOTHER'S DAY

Well, here it is-my annual Mother's Day post. In reality, this won't be an "annual" post unless I do one next year since this is the very first one. I plan to do one next year, though. If I remember...

And... I'm aware that it's late, but I thought that appropriate, since I always forget it until about a week later, despite a loving wife (Mary) who considers it her mission in life to let me know about things like this. The only problem is, she always lets me know the day before. Like I'm expected to remember it that long!

To make up for not sending a card on time, I decided to send Mom more than just one of those syrupy Hallmark cards. This year, I sent her a cassette tape of the movie, "It's a Wonderful Life" starring that irrepressible boyish Jimmy Stewart from my private collection. (This is the movie where he isn't dressed up like a giant rabbit, in which he's also irrepressible and boyish.)

Then, the second I got home from mailing it to her, I realized I'd made a grievous mistake. I hadn't sent her the movie I thought I had. It dawned on me that I'd sent her an entirely different movie. To be exact, my copy of the classic film noir, College Girls Having Monkey Sex, Part XIV. If you haven't seen it, it's the one where the coed from Vassar has her boobs pointed in opposite directions and her co-star ends up with whiplash trying to treat them equally and stay on his mark. ("Mark" for you non-theater majors is the piece of tape the director places on the floor to show the actor where to stand.)

Oops.

The reason I realized my faux pas, was that when I got home I thought I might want to watch a few minutes of it and couldn't locate it and then remembered I'd labeled it… you guessed it… It's a Wonderful Life… in the unlikely event Mary went through my collection looking for a something to watch.

I ran all the way back to the post office in hopes I could talk the mail guy into letting me have my package back, but it seems they have rules against that kind of thing. You can guess how that turned out, if you've ever had to deal with the United Nazi States of Mail Carriers. Guy treated me like I was the Unibomber. I called him "Cliff" and "Newman" but he didn't get it.

I was in a sweat when I found it had already been shipped,

but then I remembered Mom didn't have a cassette player. Or a VCR. Or, even a TV. She'd sold her TV when The Ed Sullivan Show went off the air a few years ago.

The luck of the Irish!

Realizing I better do something more than send her a tape she couldn't watch, I asked Mary if we could take her out to dinner.

"When?" she said. "On Father's Day? That's the next holiday."

I laughed. (That's it. I just laughed) Then, I said, "Of course not, silly. This weekend."

"Only if you don't use that name in the restaurant that you always do," she said.

I agreed and called Mom to give her the good news. "We'd like to take you out to dinner for your big day," I said. "Where would you like to go?"

"Would this be an early Mother's Day for 2011 or the late one for 2010?"

I laughed. (That's it. I just laughed. I've been trained by Mary.) Then I said, "Of course not, silly. The second one. 2010. The battery in my calendar died."

Golden Corral was her first choice, but I talked her out of that. "They're closed," I lied. "There was a big pileup of people on walkers and the health department closed them until they widen the ramp. Thirty-six people suffered aluminum whiplash. There are herds of lawyers everywhere and you couldn't get in even if it was open."

She sounded skeptical, but then said her second choice was Red Lobster. This, to a guy who's lived in New Orleans half his life and has actually eaten real seafood was like the chef at Ruth's Chris Steak House grabbing a square hamburger down at Wendy's on his day off, but hey, it was my mom and it was her day. I looked forward to gazing at their menu with pictures of the nine-pound lobsters on the menu and them seeing the actual three-ounce one they served. To be fair, the actual meal is the same size as the picture when you put them up next to each other.

She decided to drive down from where she lived in South Bend to our home in Ft. Wayne, a true adventure for the other drivers on the highway since she's 88 and drives older than her actual age. You've heard that saying? "(Blank) drives like old people fuck? Slow and jerky." That's Mom. If you ever see those long lines on winding country roads where there are 117 cars trailing behind the John Deere tractor, it was Mom who taught that tractor driver how to navigate our rural byways. I suggested she might want to start out the night before to get to our place on time, but she didn't think that was all that funny.

"You're not too old to get a spanking, Mr. Smartmouth," she said. Well, yes, I am, Mom. I have gray hair and arthritis and can remember when phones had dials. Besides, how are you going to catch me? I can crawl faster than you can walk. I didn't say anything like that to her, of course. After all, she's my mom and deserves respect. Besides, as long as I knew I could outrun her that was enough. I didn't have to rub it in.

Before she hung up, she said, "You're not going to use that name you always do in restaurants, are you? Because if you do, I'm not coming."

"No, Mom, I'm not. I'm grown up, now." Jesus! What do she and Mary do? Get together and compare notes?

She gets here, only two and a half hours past her ETA, and we all climb in the car and head for the gastronomical delights only available at national chains.

We get to the Red Lobster and I'm anticipating something on my plate that looks like a medium jumbo shrimp that they're going to try to pawn off as a Maine lobster and we all go in. This takes a while as we're proceeding at Mom's pace which is about as fast as the last day of school.

"We should hurry, Mom," I said. "They close in only six hours."

Mary gives me a dirty look. So does Mom, who says, "You're not too big to get a spanking." I consider showing her my driver's license to show her my age as she's obviously forgotten, but I don't. It's Mother's Day. Well, not really-that was last week, but we're operating on the theme of Mother's Day and I want to remain true to the spirit.

I hustle ahead of them and give our name to the hostess.

When I come back, Mom says, "How long?" and Mary says, "You didn't give them that name, did you?"

"Twenty minutes," I say to Mom, and to Mary I just give a pained look, as if to say, "How could you even think I'd do that?"

We pass the time listening to Mom complain about the present government and ask to see a menu so she can make her choice, which is always the same. The lobster/shrimp combo. I think she just wants to check to make sure they haven't taken either off the menu. Although, if they ran out of one, they could just serve the one that was left and tell the diner it was the missing one. Who would know?

Then, she lays a bomb on me. "I love that movie, you sent

me," she said. "I'm going over to your sister Ann's house to watch it when I get back home."

And then, our table is announced over the loudspeaker.

"Donner, party of three."

I get two dirty looks from the women I'm with.

"That's us," I say.

I love Mother's Day!

BAD NEWS

I'm afraid I have some bad news. Let me take that back. I have some terrible news. Bad news is when your wife says she's leaving you for the water softener man. This is far worse than that. This is on the level of news that she's leaving you for the guy who lives down by the river in his refrigerator carton and not taking the kids with her

Okay. Ready? Sitting down? Here goes.

It's official. Once again, I didn't win the Pulitzer Prize for Literature. How many times must I taste the bitter truth that time is running out? Once a year, I guess, until I run out.

And, what beat me out this year? The Orphan Master's Son by Adam Johnson. You're kidding, right? Here's the description:

An exquisitely crafted novel that carries the reader on an adventuresome journey into the depths of totalitarian North Korea and into the most intimate spaces of the human heart.

It's a book set in North Korea? Who the hell nominated this? Dennis Rodman? Who even reads books set in North

Korea? Even North Koreans don't read books set in North Korea. Well, that's not exactly their fault-they aren't allowed to by that sweet little cherub, Dear Leader. Speaking of cherubs, I woke up this morning with a sweet little cherub in my skivvies... Or was that a chub? Whatever. They both look the same.

I suspect it won because of the author's name. He's named after two American presidents. Jingoism at its worst.

I should have known I wouldn't win once again after last year when they couldn't find a single book to give the award to. There were only five million books published last year (even taking out the four million self-published autobiographies that really suck swamp water, that still leaves a million books, give or take a few hundred thousand.).

How can you not give one single book the award? Even the year the Miss America contestants were all dogs, they still gave the award to someone. Bert Parks took it himself one year. That was the year there weren't any brunettes from Mississippi and Georgia. But, hey-they still awarded it to somebody.

I've had it. I'm taking serious action. I've just composed a strongly-worded letter to all the judges of next year's Pulitzer committee, notifying them that I'm officially withdrawing any and all of my books from consideration. I'm sending it via Overnight Delivery, Certified Mail. That means it won't arrive in their mail boxes until August, 2015 but I have no control over that. They'll at least be aware of my sentiments.

And, as it happens, I'm outlining a new novel that fits all of their crappy requirements. It's set in (some obscure country which I haven't decided yet, but one with lots of consonants and only one vowel) and it's about the Mayor of Cracktown. It's about this guy who lives in a village with the Entering and Leaving signs on the same pole, and in this little shack with a bunch of farm animals of various religious persuasions living inside with him. He has no money (always a requirement of these kinds of books and which immediately makes him a genius). He has a major fight with the garda who have discovered he's far exceeded the legal quota of farm animals allowed in a domicile, one of which he claims shouldn't count as it's a very pretty Merino ewe to whom he's pledged his troth. He's not sure what a "troth" is but it's in a lot of Dickens' books he read as a kid so he knows it's important to pledge his.

In this book, I devote a lot of pages to his internalizing, which seems to be high on the list of stuff these Pulitzer folks look for. There's one really dazzling scene where he ponders how clichés came about and fantasizes about their origins. Like that delightful phrase "blind alley" (which, I, for one can never hear too many times.). He ruminates and ponders and rumes some more and comes to the conclusion that it originally denoted a place where German shepherds congregated en masse, waiting to be hired by the seeing-challenged (PC term for blind people) and veterans with PTSD. This riveting scene takes up 26 pages, which is guaranteed to manipulate them even more than a teenaged boy's chub during bathroom time. And, in much the same way.

One of the indoor farm animals will be a dog. His only function is to be in the book so I can use his picture on the cover and on the Intergnat. You and I know it's just a frickin' mutt, but people on the Intergnat have assigned a mystical aura to dogs and cats. You know, those critters that eat their own poop, cough up furballs and lick themselves all day long. We know that mostly they're glorified door mats, but people get all weepy about them and giggly and attribute them with the same wisdom they do old Indian guys crying over some trash on Highway 10. THEY SELL BOOKS. And influence Pulitzer judges.

The protagonist will be a creepy loner who, in real life, people would take a wide berth around when they see him with his sign begging for work outside Target, but instantly make into a wise man simply because there's a whole book centered around him and we see he thinks about pithy stuff like blind alleys. If he was so frickin' wise why ain't he a plumber's assistant or a governor or something?

My protagonist is also an orphan. And a master. And the son of a dog. This makes it a sure winner.

Yes, I could easily win next year, which makes my protest even more meaningful. I know what it takes after studying these things for ~~hours days~~ weeks. It's important to know who's handing out the hardware. The judges are elderly folks who braid the hair in their noses (the women) and meet at Golden Corral to discuss the nominated books. The men on the committee treat the books nominated the same way they do the fine wines they own. They don't open them. That would destroy their value and besides, who has to actually read the nominated book? They can learn all they want to from the glorious Intergnat. The men also have lush bushes in their noses, but they use them differently than the women (most of the women…). They weave them cleverly around their noggins kind of like the comb-overs aging sportscasters do. Along with a few well-placed strands from the ear hairs.

This is the real secret as to why my book never gets nominated. I labored for years thinking they actually read the books. Don't laugh-I bet you know at least one person in your own circle who thought the same thing. So maybe you knew, but are you willing to say that all of your friends wear those helmets and rode the short bus to H.S. and took all A.P. classes? So-cut me a break here.

The trick to getting on these judges' radar is to effectively utilize the Intergnat. Most of us writers have been sold a bill of goods about what the 'Gnat does. Social media doesn't sell books. It doesn't sell squat. It doesn't sell books-it sells social media. No one cares about your stupid book on social media. They pretend to… so you'll buy their stupid book. Writers who can't sell books have one problem-they write crappy books. Yakking about them all day long on social media sells three books total. That's it. And that's to trolls who are burning to write one-star reviews on it. When social media sells books, let me know. Otherwise, lay down by your dish with your butt-licking dog.

But, Pulitzer Prize judges do look at the Intergnat. All day long. It's why they don't have time to actually read the books themselves. Too busy Facebooking each other or Twittering about "that wonderful book about North Korea Dennis Rodman likes so well." Think about this. 1. Dennis Rodman picture with Dear Leader was on the "Gnat" one million, three hundred thousand and sixty-nine times last year. 2. A book set in North Korea won the Pulitzer. Make the connection, dummy! This ain't nuclear physics!

So, if I weren't about to withdraw from consideration,

here's what I'd do. Get me a babe to do my networking for me. As my pretend girlfriend, Lo Hai Qu so eloquently pointed out-"Blogbitches rule, blogdicks drool." Okay. I accept that. If I was going to remain involved in the competition, I'd be on my knees beseeching my pal, Anonymous 9 (Blogbitch Supreme) if she'd please help this lowly Blogdick (me) out.

But I won't. You can relax, 9. I'm out of all this. I just hope you nice folks "twit" and "face" my new book all over the Intergnat. I have but one goal for next year. That all the UPS drivers who deliver my books are forced to buy trusses.

(I hope you know this was all in fun, folks. Although, if I have to say this, it takes all the force away…) I do love the Intergnat and I truly do love the folks on here. True that. And they do sell books. Books on how to use the Intergnat to sell books…)

As John Goodman once said, "See ya in the funny papers."

Blue skies,

Les

LES EDGERTON *is an ex-con, matriculating at Pendleton Reformatory in the sixties for burglary (plea-bargained down from multiple counts of burglary, armed robbery, strong-armed robbery and possession with intent). He was an outlaw for many years and was involved in shootouts, knifings, robberies, high-speed car chases, dealt and used drugs, was a pimp, worked for an escort service, starred in porn movies, was a gambler, served four years in the Navy, and had other misadventures. He's since taken a vow of poverty (became a writer) with 18 books in print. Three of his novels have been sold to German publisher, Pulpmaster for* *the German language rights. His memoir, Adrenaline Junkie is currently being marketed.*

Keeping the Scene Alive

Angel Luis Colon

Bullet is an asshole.

Granted, it's obvious with a nickname like Bullet-displayed in gold and diamonds along the top front row of his teeth-but it takes a special kind of bastard to book a band and hold off on payment.

This is the third time we've let him do this to us. The third time we've clung to that empty hope that it would be 'different this time'. We get the call from one of the "bookers" working Bullet's piece of shit dive bar, Canarsie High, and drive down to play in front of the late shift day-drinkers and the occasional NYU freshman desperate to drink in a place that won't card them. All of that to not get a fucking dollar for our time and effort.

Maybe we're the assholes. Maybe Doom Mother are three of the most gullible, starving artist idiots to ever try and break in on the flat lined NYC thrash metal scene. We're not the best band out there, but shit, we've worked over six years to get this far. It has to count for something.

"Sorry boys, not enough bodies in the house tonight." This is his mantra now.

"It's a fucking Thursday night, Bullet. Besides that, you promised at least a c-note to make up for the last two times." Our drummer and lead singer, Vince, is our mouthpiece; Danny, the guitarist, is too busy at the bar; and me, well, I'm the bassist – I get ignored and stuck in the corner.

"Dennis." Vince says my name and I snap back into this shithole.

"Yeah?"

"How much did we lose on gas this time?"

I'm also the numbers guy. Gas, gear and weed expenses need tracking? I'm your man. "Well, shit. We drove down from Danny's this time. That's like a two hour drive. We probably dropped seventy bucks to fill the tank. The drive up will kill another half of the tank."

My van's a gas guzzling bitch like that.

"See? Almost a hundred fucking bucks, man." Vince gets in Bullet's face. Has that habit of thinking if he picks his shoulders up and goes up on his toes he'll manage to scare something out of someone. Not sure how he thinks that'll work on a man that calls himself Bullet.

I clear my throat. "You know, maybe we can set up some kind of deal-like a scheduled set of appearances with a flat fee…"

There's no use in my ideas. Bullet and Vince only have eyes for each other.

"Take it easy, Vinny. I'll tell you what I can do." He motions behind him to the bar where Danny's flirting with a bar back that can't be a day over seventeen. "I'll let you boys have a round on me."

"I don't drink," I point out.

Nobody listens.

"Are you fucking crazy? Three times, Bullet, three fucking times. You know what?" Vince settles back on his heels and throws his hands up. "We're fucking done man. Next time you hear from me, it's through my lawyer."

We don't have a lawyer.

"That what your daddy does?" Bullet smirks and calls the bluff like a god damn pro. That grill of his shines brighter than any of the low wattage bulbs he's got clinging to life in the ancient fixtures lining the ceilings. He slides his eyes over to me. "See, you need to be more like Dennis. He keeps his fucking yap shut and plays. I bet his dad is an engineer or a fucking scientist – something with half a brain." He points a sausage finger at me. "Right?"

I nod. "Well, he's a line technician…"

"That doesn't fucking matter." Vince's ears are red.

"Course it matters. Good father's all the difference between a good kid like Dennis and a fucking whiney little twat like you." He laughs and lights a Pall Mall. "When did your Daddy walk out on you and your mommy?" He's read Vince from the first time he shafted us. Now it's a game to him.

Daddy issues are Vince's forte, so I know to step in and hold him back. He makes a good show of it, but Bullet just stares at him and smiles like he's watching a puppy nip at his hand. There's this emptiness in his eyes that shakes me. Seems I'm the only one that feels it.

"Fuck's sake, Vince." Danny's watching from his little love

perch at the bar. The bar back's on his lap now. "Bullet, I'll take the free round. Fuck those two."

"I don't drink," I repeat.

"I know." Danny gives me that devil's smile of his and goes back to making the teen queen giggle against his chest.

"See, not all of you are whiners. Your boy over there knows to take what he gets."

Vince is fuming and pulls against me-not with much effort. He finally quits and groans. "Fine, but this is the last time, man. You want Doom Mother to play your shit hole – you gotta pay."

Bullet's already ten feet away and headed to his office downstairs. "Whatever you say, kid, whatever you say."

Vince walks to the bar and motions to the bartender. "Long Island Ice Tea. Might as well have something expensive if that's my pay." He turns to Danny. "What are you having?"

"Bud."

"Yeah, and two Buds for my friend down there."

"Vince?" I tap his shoulder.

He ignores me again.

"Vince?"

"What?"

"Order me a soda, I gotta hit the head."

"Yeah, whatever." He turns back to the bar and takes a sip of his cocktail. There's a beat of silence and then he grimaces. "What is this shit, you go to fucking bartending school, man?"

Danny and Vince are busy, so I make my way towards the bathroom, but take a last minute turn to the stairs that lead down to Bullet's office. It's pitch black down there, but I go down either way. It's time for me to do the talking-maybe work out a solid deal and keep bridges from burning.

I walk in on Bullet getting head from some other girl that looks younger than Danny's bar back. There's a stack of twenties and hundreds in front of him. The whole thing looks like a back-alley production of a Bond villain scene.

"What the fuck do you want?" Bullet doesn't let her stop servicing him. I can see his arm flex as he pushes her head down. He raises an eyebrow. "You gonna stand there and watch? Crank one out? Fucking scram."

I turn and head right back up the stairs. At the bar, Vince has finished his drink. There's no soda for me.

"Did you ask for my soda?"

Vince stamps a foot and sighs. "Let's go before I burn this fucking place to the ground. Get Danny, I'm going outside."

Danny's at the end of the bar now, making out with his new friend. I take a deep breath and walk over. A few steps before I'm in talking range, he holds a hand up and breaks away from her long enough to get some air. "I'm cool, got a ride already."

"Great…" Whatever, I'm fed up too.

I walk outside and the sun is still out. I check my watch and it's only a quarter to eight. My chest feels a little tight, so I take a hit off my inhaler.

What kind of band is done with their set at a quarter to fucking eight?

"Bullet called." Vince barges into my house like the wacky fucking neighbor in a sitcom.

"So?" I'm busy watching TV.

"So pack up, we got a gig tonight."

I sit up. "Wait, what? It's a Tuesday, Canarsie closes early on Tuesdays."

Vince paces around the room and lights a cigarette. "What's the problem?"

"Well, for one, you said we weren't doing anymore gigs for Bullet – that we'd be better off focusing on studio time."

"We can do both."

"Will there be money this time?"

Vince stops the pacing and looks over to me. "Bullet and I squashed that shit. We're good to go."

"Alright...glad to hear that, but there's a bit of a hitch."

'What's that?" He exhales an ungodly amount of smoke my way. Obviously, my asthma never counts for much.

"I'm on call tonight."

"For that firefighter bullshit? It's fucking voluntary, man-not even a real job. Shit, can you even make it up a flight of stairs without keeling over? What the fuck are the requirements to even join that shit – show up? The minute they find out you've got that inhaler you're out on your ass."

Now he remembers the asthma. I feel my face flush and my ears get hot. "We're not arguing about this shit again. I'm on call. Can't play and you can't get a ride from me." I turn the TV off and stand up. "Call Barry to cover for me, he knows most of the new stuff."

Vince scowls. "You won't get paid then."

That's actually funny. "Tell you what; Bullet actually comes through with anything more than another free round for you gullible motherfuckers, I'll pay for the next three studio sessions." I have to hand it to Vince – we're such a terrible band that only a single dive bar will book us and we're such a sad set of assholes, that same bar hangs us out to dry without batting an eye.

True rock and roll, ladies and gents.

Still, I appreciate Vince's passion. Pretty sure Danny and I would have been long gone if he wasn't so hell bent on whatever making whatever fantasies flittering in the vacuum of his head come true. Doom Mother is all his. The logo, the "image" – everything – Danny and I are just the side-talent. Any suggestions are noted and immediately ignored. I like to think Vince would make a phenomenal middle manager if he only had the connections.

"So it's a hard no?" Vince puts out his cigarette in a glass of water I hadn't finished.

"Just about, brother. If I get out early, I can try to pick you guys up. If we get a call, all bets are off."

"Aw, yeah, I'm sure you guys will have so many things to do – so many fucking lives to save. In the meantime, you're shitting on our chance, man. The scene is fucking dying."

"Vince, the thrash metal scene's been dead for decades – with an "s", man – decades."

"Bullshit."

That's about the best argument he's ever going to have against that point.

"Well, dude, I gotta shower and sort my ass out. You need anything else?"

"Nah…" He lights another god damn cigarette. "I see where we're at." Vince struts out like he's making a point. Don't ask me what the fuck it is.

I could set my god damn watch to when Vince was going to call – quarter to eight exactly. "That motherfucker," he screams into the receiver of the 'Unknown Number' that dialed me up. I figure it's the payphone on the corner of Saint Mark's Place.

"How was the free drink?" I'm caught up playing spider solitaire on the firehouse's only working computer.

"Fuck off. Barry ran off after the arguing started. We need a ride."

"Can you wait about an hour and change?"

He grunts. "Yeah, I'll grab some pizza. The bar's already shut down for whatever inventory bullshit that asshole said he needed to do."

"I can't understand what made you think a gig on a Tuesday night would lead to. Anyway, Danny need a ride too?"

"Any gig is a gig." God bless him, he still thinks we're fated to be something – anything. "And fuck Danny, he'll find some ditz to do him a solid-he always does."

A few of the guys come rolling in from washing the truck outside. I wave at them with a smile. "Okay, so I'll probably get down there around nine thirty. Just chill out, eat and get your head straight, okay?"

"Yeah…yeah I can do that. It's just…"

The house bell cuts him off.

"Oh, shit, look…I gotta run." I hang up the phone and jump up to my feet. The handful of us all dart our eyes to one another for a split second – it's our first real call.

Vince will have to wait.

††††

I drive into the city still covered in soot and half my gear tossed all over the car. It's after midnight and I keep redialing Vince – no dice. I'm still buzzing on adrenaline and the pride of not having to use my inhaler. When I check my phone, there are thirty texts from Vince.

Some of the highlights:

Dude, you on your way?

Where teh fuck r u?

Fuck this.

Going into Canarsie adn getting money.

That last one worries the shit out of me. Not because Vince has a habit of causing trouble that's way out of his league – he does – but because a guy like Bullet is more than willing to take him up on that cause. Sure, he's an asshole and the whole nickname/grill thing is near comic book villain shit, but he has a rep of living up to some of that crazy he likes to advertise.

I swing my car up to the curb in front of Canarsie's. All the lights are out. Maybe they finished up with the Tuesday night inventory – maybe Vince missed them too. I hop out of the car and get over to the front door when the paranoia hits me and I backtrack to my rear driver's side door. I get it open and grab my pike pole. Maybe it's overkill, but there's this cold feeling in my gut that won't let go. With this in my hands, it goes away – a little.

The front door is open and I hear nothing inside. That gets my heart pumping. There's barely light, just the faint glow of neon reminding me that beer or a shot of Jager would be awesome about now. Not three steps towards the stairway that leads to Bullet's office and I find him.

Bullet's leaned against the wall opposite the stairs and he's in a state. The lack of light hides the worst of it, but his face is banged up bad and his button down looks soaked with something darker than water. He's got a revolver in his right hand. I edge up to him slow and give him a poke with the blunt end of my pike.

No response.

"Shit," I say under my breath. There's shuffling downstairs in the office. I ignore it and scramble to turn the lights on. I ignore the mess that Bullet's in, but a single glance confirms he's shuffled off to somewhere else –hopefully hot.

No, that's terrible. Shouldn't think that way.

"Hello?" I call out, hoping it's Vince or Danny – someone I know. "I've, uh, I've got a weapon."

There's more shuffling followed by a groan. It's familiar enough to put less fear than urgency in me, so I double time it down the stairs. I find the lights down there and the office is a mess of scattered papers and overturned furniture. I notice the trail of blood leading from a chair and up the stairs to where Bullet took his final breath. Dead center of the room is Vince, sprawled out on his back and taking slow, shallow gulps of air. His eyes are wide and there's a hole in his chest that seems a mile wide and a few feet deep. There's a broken vodka bottle in his hand-the business end thick with blood.

"Aw, fuck." I drop the pike and go to him. When I touch him, he's cold as fucking ice – not much time left. "Vince, come on." My hands fumble for my phone and I go to dial 911. Vince nearly kills me with fright when he snatches the phone away.

"No! Just go!" He takes another gulp of the stale, beer

stained air.

"Dude, are you fucking nuts, you need medical attention."

"The band!" He's in shock.

"That doesn't matter right now. Give me the phone." I go for it and he somehow musters the strength to throw it towards the stairs.

"It's okay," he whispers. His eyes close and he's done.

I try to run through all my emergency training – the blood stoppage, the CPR-but I draw a blank. It's all in there, but the shock's just knocked it all out of me. Besides, Vince is long gone. He made the call – these are the consequences.

I stand and find a towel draped over one of the chairs – collect my pike and phone too. I use the towel to wipe down whatever I've touched as I make my way back upstairs. Bullet's a lump-an old pile of rotting meat that doesn't seem so scary anymore. I walk over and open his mouth, hook my fingers just under the palate and pull down. His grill pops out with a wet pop. I wipe it off and slip it into my pocket.

Enough time spent in this shit hole – I make tracks to the car and get the fuck out of there. Ten blocks down, I make an anonymous call on a payphone about screams at Canarsie High. I figure that gives me time to get home and get in a shower.

Pretty sure there won't be sleep.

Danny gives me a call a few days later. "Dude, what the fuck happened?"

I give him the parts of the story he needs to know. How I

had to work late and Vince decided to collect on what was due to Doom Mother. Only part that didn't need repeating was my visit. I'd have to carry that by myself.

He doesn't speak much, just gives the 'yeahs' and 'rights' that come with conversations like this.

I get to the meat. "So, about Doom Mother. Guess we call it quits?"

"Well, I was sort of calling about that. Guy I know in the Bowery is pretty interested in having us. I figure I can convince Barry to come down. You could sing all of Vince's parts."

"Dude, isn't it kind of soon?"

"Well, yeah, but people are really fucking responding to this. My boy said the turnout might be huge. Real kickstart for the scene, you know?"

I catch myself smiling. "You know what? Sure. I think Vince would have been all about that."

"Absolutely."

"What time's the show?"

"After ten. It's a good slot."

"Great, I'll talk to you then."

"Oh, and Dennis?"

"Yeah?"

"I can drive if you want."

"Sounds good to me." I hang up.

On my desk, Bullet's grill sits-sparkling under the sunlight that spills through the windows. I pick it up and run my finger through the grooves between each letter – let it fall into the wastebasket at my feet.

Angel Luis Colon *is the author of the novella, 'The Fury of Blacky Jaguar'. His Derringer nominated fiction has appeared in multiple web and print journals and he's written for sites like My Bookish Ways, The Life Sentence, and The LA Review of Books. He's also an editor for Shotgun Honey, home of some of the best hard-boiled flash fiction on the web. The next time he updates his bio, he hopes to be shilling his debut novel, 'Hell Chose Me', currently repped by Foundry Literary + Media.*

Lucha

Jack Getze

Lucha spilled nude from the king-size bed. She collected her panties, the Diane von Furstenberg black evening dress, high heel shoes and her too-big-for-a-reason, sequined clutch bag, carried these things low against her thigh in a parade to the hotel suite's marble bathroom. She held her chin high and her sprouting bare breasts thrust forward, the sexy walk a final morsel of well-paid-for entertainment.

Being a slave and a prostitute killed most young women, the ones Lucha had known anyway. Drugs mainly, but she'd seen murder, disease, accident and suicide. She'd survived by lashing out at those who would abuse her, staying off drugs and accepting her bad luck – if she had to be a whore, and she did for now, she might as well be a successful one. Being habitually requested by whales made Lucha a top earner, and in Master Soo's house, that meant semi-private quarters, better food, nicer clothes and professional health care.

When Lucha came out of the bathroom minutes later, the von Furstenberg covering her athletic body, the straight ebony hair brushed to a shine, her internal warning bells pealed like

Christmas mass at St. Patrick's. While she'd been dressing, the first john had invited another man into the room -- the new guy sullen, mean in the eyes and dirty. Soiled clothes. Yellow teeth.

"Who told you to get dressed?" the first john said.

Two men were trouble, reason enough to go edgy, but in response to the first john's comment, the second guy produced a sick sneer that zapped Lucha into full alert. Adrenaline exploded in her blood. Her taut, nineteen-year-old body prepared to run or, as she preferred, to fight – lucha being the Spanish word for fight, a nickname first substituted for Lucia by another Hispanic girl one year earlier.

"My friend just wants a taste," the john said.

No doubt. Lucha guessed the new prick could only get laid if cash were involved. And lots of it. But she saved her scorn, fought the chemicals pumping inside her and offered the two creeps no reaction at all while she considered her options, focusing her empty eyes on the container of fresh flowers that decorated a table. The scene reminded her of a Van Gogh painting she'd seen last week in a full-page Vogue magazine ad - bright, mustard-colored iris stuffed in a sky-blue Chinese vase.

The first john growled like a dog. "Hey, bitch, I asked you a question. Who told you to get dressed? And you shouldn't mind taking care of my friend, not for the pile of money I paid you."

Lucky for them Lucha already had her cash. It was a good rule of Master Soo's; payment first, sex second, and this john's wad of hundreds was already tucked inside her black sequined clutch. Right next to her SOG Seal 2000, a scary looking knife she now touched for reassurance. It had been several months since Lucha had needed to threaten a client with it.

"I'm sorry, but I must leave," she said. "Master Soo has scheduled another appointment for me tonight. Perhaps if you call, I could come back later."

She put her long legs in motion, smiling at the first john as she strode past the second. She hated men, wanted to slice off every dick and testicle she'd ever laid hands on. Men were nothing but pricks, essentially. Talking pricks or quiet pricks. Tall ones, short ones. Fat and skinny. But dicks every one. And there was nothing worse than a mean one, the kind of coward who hurt women. Lucha had suffered her share of abuse over the past four years, but twice-weekly martial arts training and a big knife usually changed a coward's mind.

The SOG Seal 2000 was twelve inches long. Two-hundred bucks on eBay.

Neither john seemed in a hurry to stop her progress toward the doorway, and by the time Lucha touched the brass door handle, she figured the solid oak wasn't going to open. When she tried anyway, to make sure, the two johns laughed like teenagers. A steel wedge had been jammed solidly between the rug and the door. Testing the obstacle with her foot, she knew immediately that to free herself, she'd have to get down on one knee and dig at the wedge with her knife. Instead, she swung to face them.

The first john lay stretched on the bed, one hand concealed under rumpled white sheets. The second prick remained in his chair with a view of the choppy, green and white Atlantic Ocean. The view, the suite and the fresh flowers meant the first john was rich -- like most of her clients these days. She'd advanced quickly in Master Soo's stable since finally growing breasts. She could pass for twelve or twenty-six now, watch TV cartoons or order cocktails in classy A.C. or New York restaurants. Whatever the johns wanted. Whatever the pricks were willing to pay for.

"I need to leave," Lucha said. "Master Soo will be worried."

These guys and their laughter made her scalp crawl with imaginary caterpillars. After spending four of her nineteen years making pricks happy, Lucha could look at a john and know important things, and she did not like what she saw, especially the new arrival. The man with soiled clothes and dirty teeth. His laughter reminded Lucha of a snake's hiss.

The new prick stood and stretched as tall as he could now, making a circus show for Lucha how big he was, puffing out his chest, inflating himself. Being a man. Being a prick. "Take off your clothes," he said. The words came out like a snarl.

This second prick was over six feet and had to weigh two-forty. But he was plump and lazy, too, the way he skipped exercise and personal hygiene. His fingernails, the hair, skin, those yellow teeth – everything was filthy. Probably a drinker, too, those red lines on his cheeks; the kind of man who couldn't keep a job.

She reached inside her black clutch. "I want to leave, gentlemen. Now."

"Bitch," the second prick said. Maybe correctly guessing Lucha's purse contained a weapon, he came fast at her, his right hand clenched. Anger contorted his face. Maybe pleasure, too. He couldn't wait to hit her.

She hopped left and did what she did hundreds of times every week -- produced a practiced right front kick. This one caught her attacker square in the junk. He screamed and dropped to one knee, his hands grabbing his crotch. The collision pushed Lucha backward, but she kept her balance and her hand on the SOG 2000, not an easy trick in her three-inch heeled Valentines with a pointed toe.

Movement turned her focus: The first john crawled across the rumpled bed sheets with something in his hand. The same guy she'd earlier let fill her orifices with his condom-covered penis now aimed a semiautomatic pistol at her.

"Let's start again," he said. "Take your clothes off."

His lips shifted and parted, but it was the gun talking to Lucha. The muzzle changed position haphazardly, aiming first at her face and then her breasts. When the pure black hole lined up with her own stare, Lucha shivered with the chill of death.

She ignored the fear and drooped her eyelids, Lucha trying to copy Bette Davis in the old black and white movie she'd seen three times; Bette leaving all male observers clueless as to her true intent. The two men in the suite would abuse her badly if she gave in now, probably tie her up and beat her. Maybe worse. She'd sensed cruelty during his sex, now savagery in the first john's weapon. The second prick still knelt on the carpet, groaning and catching his breath. But he'd rally in another minute or two, and he might be evil enough to torture and kill her.

The first john pushed the gun closer to her face. "I said take off your clothes – now!" He pressed his finger against the trigger.

Lucha would not be tortured. She'd rather take a bullet trying to kill these pricks. She kept one hand inside her purse but used the other to unbutton the top of her von Furstenberg, spreading her lips into a coy smile. Inching closer to the bed and the gun. Bette Davis eyes. She relaxed her body, introducing surrender to the way she carried her hips and her shoulders. She kept the act going until the prick relaxed and grinned at her.

She hopped forward, snaking the knife from her clutch, throwing her elbow at him with the same motion. Her quickness surprised him. Before he could understand and fire, Lucha had blocked his gun hand and launched her ten-ounce knife. Fully extending herself in the backhand throw, the sharp, clip-point blade began its journey only inches from the john's neck. There was no discernable swish of air, only a thud of penetration and his odd cry.

The scream became a gurgle when air bubbles mixed with the blood pumping into his throat. The bright red color and the john's exaggerated, bug-eyed gape made Lucha think briefly of a comic book cover. She clasped the knife's handle, pushed the blade deeper, then twisted her wrist when she pulled the steel out. His blood pressure zeroed. The john rolled from his bed to the carpet, a wad of soiled sheets sliding off with him. His eyes stared at some distant terror.

Lucha spun to the second john, her SOG knife ready. She pointed at his Adam's apple, the prick still on his knee, mouth and eyes wide at the sight of Lucha's attention. He crawled backward as she strode closer, the big dick trying to melt into a corner, tucking his six-foot frame against the sofa and the wall.

Lucha pulled in her air slowly. Though elevated, her pulse was not as fast as when she exercised. She'd never killed anyone before, but now that she had, well ... apparently murder didn't bother her much. Watching this second prick trying to hide in plain sight, she wanted to kill him, too.

She counted to ten and decided one death was enough. Master Soo would be angry already, but she'd be in a reckless mood if Lucha killed this second man without need. Time to burn out of this hell. She wiped her knife clean on the bed sheets and headed for the wedge-blocked doorway. When she strode past the table with the blue vase, Lucha kicked the closest wooden leg. The bouquet of yellow iris spilled across the beige carpet.

She called Master Soo on her way to the elevator. She only got on the line after Lucha had told her story first to her assistant.

"You are unhurt? Is this true?" Master Soo said.

Alone in the hotel's polished-brass elevator, Lucha touched L for Lobby. "I'm not injured, no."

"Mom Chin said you sounded unusually upset."

Master Soo's words almost made her smile. To most of Soo's girls, and apparently Soo's assistant Mom Chin as well, Lucha always sounded a little upset. "A man is dead, Master Soo, but I assure you I'm not harmed."

"Physically, perhaps. But if it's true you killed one of our clients, you could be in shock. There are other kinds of damage to be considered. You must let me send someone. Where are you now?"

Lucha's heart rate jumped. She focused on controlling her

breathing. In Master Soo's words, Lucha detected a potential new threat, a danger much greater than pricks with guns. Other kinds of damage could include many things in Master Soo's world. Though a fair employer, even kind to her best girls, Master Soo was a ruthless business woman.

"A doctor should examine you," Soo said. "Now again, where are you?"

When the elevator doors revealed a bustling, anonymous lobby, Lucha considered running away. She'd been making preparations to escape since the day she'd arrived, acquiring various bits of knowledge, saving money, becoming physically fit. Her development was not complete, her online savings inadequate, but Master Soo's reaction to the night's events could make long-term preparation unimportant.

"I'll be having coffee at a boardwalk restaurant," she said. "Sitting outside, two blocks down from the hotel."

✝✝✝

Two deformed Newport cigarettes offered buried treasure inside Lucha's sequined clutch. She was squishing out the second butt when Master Soo's black Cadillac limo turned the corner and parked against the curb. Lucha had done more than smoke while waiting.

She sipped her chocolate latte again before standing, left a twenty-dollar bill for the Asian woman who cleaned off tables and went out of her way to show Lucha a bathroom with privacy. The twenty earned her a toothy smile, honest happiness that made Lucha grin, too. She crossed thirty yards of boardwalk mentally going over her plans, imagining what could happen, depending on which assistant Soo assigned. Mom Chin was the nice one. La Rowe was Soo's enforcer. Lucha had survived a fatal appointment, but a rich client had not. She needed to be prepared for trouble.

Live rock n' roll from a different hotel lobby played out onto the busy boardwalk. A group of suit-and-tie businessmen watched her walk by, Lucha matching her stride to the music's slow, steady back-beat all the way to Master Soo's limo. A familiar face rolled down the driver's window and nodded: Alfonzo was Master Soo's personal driver, her bodyguard. Had the big boss come herself?

Lucha reached for the rear door, but Alfonzo growled. "Wait. I need to look in your purse. Master Soo came herself."

Alfonzo tumbled out of the stretched black limo like a bag of sharp sticks, his arms as long as his corn-stalk legs. An ex-boxer who'd stopped working out a decade earlier, the five-year-old Cuban was one of very few men Lucha tolerated. He'd been kind once without wanting a return favor.

She offered him her sequined clutch and whispered. "Did Master Soo say why she came?"

Alfonzo didn't answer or even look up, digging instead inside her clutch bag, finding nothing. That he wouldn't glance at her was a bad sign. So was taking her cellphone. "Where's that Navy SEAL knife of yours?" he said.

"Stuck inside the john," Lucha said. "I couldn't get it out."

Alfonzo stared at her. He didn't believe her. He know how much she'd paid for the SOG. "I need to search you then."

"You don't believe me?"

"I do, sure. But Soo wants me to make sure."

"I didn't hear her say anything."

"You know Soo and her rules." Alfonzo grabbed her waist and worked his way up, pressing his hands flat against her body, absorbing every curve and ripple of her front, back, arms and neck. When he squatted in front of her and slipped his fingers under her dress, hands around her left thigh, she winced and pulled back slightly.

"Sorry." She giggled. "I'm ticklish."

Alfonzo kept working, but not with the same degree of thoroughness. On the right side, reluctant to touch her ticklish thigh and buttocks, Soo's bodyguard didn't reach far enough under the Von Furstenberg.

Lucha clutched at her dress as she scrambled inside. The passenger compartment was dark, private and privileged. The softest of leathers. The shiniest of chrome. She sat facing forward, across the aisle from Master Soo. She watched the back of Alfonso's head through a glass partition.

"Master Soo," she said. "I am honored."

She nodded. "Lucha."

Soo was thin and firm for a woman in her sixties. A softly lighted console on her left was filled with glasses and wine bottles. Soo poured short splashes of something red in a burgundy-shaped bottle and offered Lucha one.

"A toast to your good fortune," Soo said. "Thank the gods you were not hurt."

She lifted her glass and drank, so Lucha did too, the wine sharp on her lips and tongue. She did not enjoy alcohol but unpleasant sensations could be managed.

"How could you be sure the client would not shoot you?" Soo said.

"It didn't matter. I was ready to die. They would have

tortured and killed me."

"An interesting decision. So you killed him when he threatened you?" Soo asked.

"Yes. To save my life."

Master Soo drank. "With these skills you seem so eager to display, surely you could have sliced his arm instead, taken the gun away. He is – was – a client. And a client with important friends. I have already received a phone call about this matter in addition to your own."

"Who?"

"Representatives of the second guest in the hotel room. The man whose testicle you quite literally crushed. His employer is quite unhappy. Feverish, in fact. Those two men work for a very powerful man in Manhattan."

"You're scaring me Master Soo." Lucha inched closer to the console, better hiding her thigh. She touched her dress and kept her hand there.

"You are in great demand and my highest earning employee," Soo said. "You are dependable and honest, the only person besides Mom Chin I can trust to keep her word. I am sorry to see you leave, but I have decided your departure is the best course."

Lucha's body shrank. What was Soo saying? "You sold me?"

"For quite a large sum, I must admit. To the man from Manhattan."

Lucha stared at her boss. How could she? "They'll torture and kill me. That second man wants revenge."

"Perhaps, but unlikely. The sum is too large to spend on revenge. I explained your income-producing abilities in great detail before arriving at the purchase price, believe me. He knows he can earn back his investment in—"

Lucha lunged across the space between them, the clip-point of her SOG Seal 2000 leading the way. Master Soo's arm tried to block her, but Soo was too slow. The seven-inch blade half disappeared into her chest, sliding between two ribs. Lucha pushed the blade deeper, twisting.

Something grabbed her neck -- Alfonzo, reaching through the limo's sliding window. Lucha latched onto Alfonzo's forearm, tried to unlock his grip and pull away, but he was too strong. Those skinny muscles must be like wire. He held her like a vise.

Lucha pulled her legs across the aisle and onto Soo's lap. Bracing her feet against the door frame, she pushed off, banging Alfonzo's forearm against the window's steel frame. A bone snapped. He screamed.

People walked by on the boardwalk, a woman bending and staring, trying to look inside, but the windows in Master Soo's limos were smoked nearly black.

Lucha squeezed Alfonzo's broken limb and pulled his arm and shoulder through the window. He screamed again, his contorted face close to her own.

She continued to hold Alfonzo's arm as she pulled her knife from Master Soo's quiet chest. Alfonzo had presented her with a gift once, a novel to read when she'd gotten the flu last year. Maybe she should let him live.

But Alfonzo was a witness and a prick. No matter what else men became, how nice they might act, at heart they were all pricks.

Lucha sliced his neck.

A former reporter for both the Los Angeles Times and Los Angeles Herald-Examiner, **Jack Getze** *is Fiction Editor for Anthony nominated Spinetingler Magazine, one of the internet's oldest websites for noir, crime, and horror short stories. His Austin Carr Mysteries BIG NUMBERS, BIG MONEY, BIG MOJO and the upcoming BIG SHOES are published by Down and Out Books. His short stories have appeared in A Twist of Noir, Beat to a Pulp, The Big Adios and Passages.*

Snow Joke

Tess Makovesky

"You coming or not?" said Stu. He watched the snow hurtle down like a million feathers from a thousand ripped quilts, settling in great white drifts around his feet. It had been snowing for hours, it was cold and wet, and it showed no signs of stopping this side of Christmas. Hardly the best time to go out on a job, but needs must, as they said.

His mate Benny eyed the snow in turn. "I dunno, mate. Are you sure about this?"

"Yeah. Told you. Trish's best friend said. She's married to that copper, Brian something in Traffic, and she had it straight from him. And he'd hardly tell lies if he's a copper, now would he?" That was crap, of course. He'd known a few members of the police force in his time and he could think of lots of reasons why they would lie. Not least to get him, Stu, to confess to things he had (or sometimes hadn't) done. But hopefully Benny wouldn't work that out.

Benny shrugged. "Where d'you wanna go?"

"Well, not round here. Too bleedin' obvious, innit?"

"But if we go any further we might get the van stuck in

the snow. It's already a foot deep."

"So we walk."

"You what?"

"You know, walk. Put one bleedin' leg in front of the other. You've got legs, haven't you?"

"Yeah, yeah, keep your hair on, I know what walking is. But how are we supposed to carry stuff back? Won't be worth taking much. I'm not wading through three feet of snow with a load of tellies on my back."

Stu paused and sucked a knuckle. He'd grazed it the other night pasting some bloke who'd come on to Trish in the Spotted Dog, and it was still giving him grief. It was his own fault; Trish was a stunner and you could hardly blame the opposition for getting hooked. Dead from the waist down, they'd have to be, not to eye up her particular brand of assets - assets that he himself had paid to have enhanced. "So we take the van nearer where we're going and walk the rest," he said at last. "Even you can manage that."

"I dunno, mate, the roads are going to be hell. Why are you so worked up about this anyway? It's not like we can't wait a few weeks."

He sucked his knuckle again. Benny was being difficult, and would have to be placated with the truth. "If you must know I'm a bit skint. That op for Trish didn't come cheap - I'm still paying off the bill and I've got nothing left. I can't even buy my own wife a pressie for Christmas. So are you in or not?"

"Yeah, all right, I'm in. Just remind me again what Trish's friend said."

"Trish said Gail said Brian said that it was all down to

health and safety. Said word had come down from the top brass - they're not allowed to respond to call-outs when it snows. Trish said did that mean you could get away with murder whenever the roads are bad and Gail said 'more or less'. Think about it, Benny. If they can't come out, they can't nab you if some bugger dials 999. We could do half the houses on that posh new estate and no one would ever know."

Benny stamped his feet up and down, crunching the snow beneath his size twelve boots. "I'll get the van keys," he said.

They got lost on the way because the streets all looked the same under their billowing blanket of snow. The street signs and name plates were covered up; trees and rooftops took on a fairytale look; the pavements merged with the roads. Stu clung to bits of the dashboard as Benny fought to control the van with varying degrees of success. "For fuck's sake," he snarled as they slithered into a hedge for the second time. Then he wished he'd kept quiet as Benny took both hands off the wheel to shrug.

"You think you can do any better, be my guest. I told you the roads would be bad."

Finally, navigating more by lemming-sense than skill, they arrived at the gated estate that backed onto Sutton Park. The gates were electric and at least eight feet high; Benny got out of the driver's seat and stared. "How're we going to get through them?"

"Ah, well, that's where I'm clever, see. I thought of everything. Me Mam's ex-boyfriend works the local milkman's round and knows all the tradesman's codes. All we have to do is put the number in the box and we're in." He suited action to words and the gates swung silently apart.

Benny whistled, the thin sound carrying above the howling wind. "Blimey. If I'd known it was that easy...."

"Never mind standing with your mouth open like a guppy fish - there's houses to be robbed."

They chose the first house that had no lights switched on and shoved their way through a side-gate to the back. Stu could hardly believe their luck when he spotted the half-open window above their heads. "Will you look at that. Window open even in this weather. Some folk want their heads examining."

Benny just grunted and propped the ladder they'd lugged from the van against the wall. Stu scrambled up it while Benny held it steady below. Normally they'd both go in, but it kept slipping on the snow and neither of them wanted to be half way up it when it fell.

The window looked out from a bathroom and there was nothing worth nicking in there, unless the gold taps were really gold. Stu spared them a glance and decided it wasn't worth the effort of freeing them from the bath; besides which he'd end up with water everywhere, including his brand new jeans. The next room, though, was a goldmine - pure heaven from a burglar's point of view. An iPod on the dresser, stacks of jewellery in a pretty box, cash rolled up in a sock. He lifted the lot, then took the banister-sliding route downstairs. In the kitchen he helped himself to a mince pie from the fridge, unlocked the back door and rejoined his mate outdoors.

"That was quick," said Benny, lowering the ladder and brushing loose snow off its rungs.

"Yeah, well, I don't hang about. Besides, I only took the small stuff - like you said, it's too much hard work lugging tellies and stuff back to the van." He licked pastry off his fingers and remembered not to wipe them on his jeans. "C'mon, then, where next?"

The next house wasn't so forgiving with its windows and they had to smash a pane with a brick. Stu thought the row would bring a nest of neighbours round their heads but after a breathless wait it all seemed quiet enough. They hopped inside and raided the stack of presents under the tree. One of them turned out to be a sled - flat-bed shape recognisable even under reams of gift wrap - so they piled everything else on that and took their ill-gotten gains for a winter wonderland ride.

Just before they left Stu smelled booze and tracked it down to a decanter of sherry, presumably left out for Santa Clause. He took a swig straight from the bottle and smacked his lips. "Good stuff, that."

Benny frowned. "Good job you're not driving. The roads are bad enough out there without you getting pissed."

"Yeah well I'm not," said Stu, draining the decanter before fumbling with the catch on the door. His fingers weren't working properly, no doubt because of the cold.

Their luck faded at the next house they tried, which was locked up like Fort Knox. Stu decided that discretion was better than being fried by an electric trip-wire or lasered to the wall. "Sod that for a game of soldiers," he said, and they vaulted the fence and went next door.

This time they hit the jackpot. The house was filled to bursting with presents that hadn't yet been wrapped. There were chocolates and smellies and expensive toys, jewellery and watches and electronic gadgets galore. "Fuck me," said

Benny, whistling. "They've only ordered the entire contents of the Argos catalogue."

They added what they could to the pile on the sled and Benny found some twine to lash it down. Stu, meanwhile, was stuffing his face with the chocolates, even though they were nuts which he didn't usually like.

Benny's frown became a full-blown scowl. "Keep that up and you'll be too fat to run away."

"Run away from what? I told you the police won't be out tonight. Not if it's snowing, I said, and it could hardly snow harder if it tried."

"Yeah, well, you just never know," said Benny.

"Not getting cold feet, are you?"

The effect wasn't quite what he expected, as Benny's disapproval turned into a guffaw. "Ha ha - cold feet in this weather! Get it? You know, they're cold because of the snow. Ha!"

"Ah, shut up and take this lot back to the van. I'm going to check out the houses further down the street."

Outside it was coming down thicker than ever, with tiny flakes that danced and whirled. Stu watched his mate trudge off with the sled and thought it looked like coke at a disco if someone had kicked over the stash. Quite pretty, really, if you were into that sort of thing. He stood with his mouth open, watching flake after flake descend. Definitely pretty, and so soft and quiet. So very, very quiet. He could almost lie down here, wrap himself in the soft white folds and drift off into sleep.

"Stu!" came a yell and he jolted back awake. What the hell?

More shouts, and general scuffling about, and he could

see some figures jostling at the other end of the road. Even as he watched cars with flashing lights drew up and more figures scrambled out. Two of them began to run towards him, and again he heard Benny's despairing yell. "Stu! Run for it!" Against all the odds, the police had answered someone's call.

The cars had blocked his only escape route; the road the other way just led deeper into the estate. But the street lights bathed the snow in a weird orange glow and showed him another way out - the houses to his right backed straight onto Sutton Park. Dark trees and bushes beckoned; in that vast wilderness there'd be plenty of places to hide. And if he was quick, the pursuing police might not see where he'd gone.

He shot down a driveway and scrambled over a fence, then waded towards the nearest stand of trees. He'd been to the Park once before, on a Sunday afternoon with his ex and her three kids; they'd kicked a football about, eaten ice-creams and paddled in one of the ponds. It had seven lakes, two golf courses and its own Roman road and had seemed colossal even then, in bright sunshine with hordes of other folk about. In the dark, with the confusing blur of snow, it was like a whole new foreign land. Narnia, perhaps, or Lapland where the reindeer were. He half expected one to appear right now, its antlers draped with tinsel with Father Christmas in tow. But there was no sign of life, no lights, no signposts, nothing to tell him which way to go. In minutes he knew he was lost. He began to have misgivings, closely followed by second thoughts. Blunder around for too long and he could vanish without trace; his bones might be found when this snow thawed, then again they might not. The easiest thing would be to follow his footsteps back to where he'd come in, and take his chances with the police. He could always hang about near the fence until they got bored and went home. They'd be unlikely to see or hear him in this.

For a while it worked, but he'd forgotten about the snow. It was still falling thickly and covering up his footprints as fast as he could follow them. Soon they would disappear and he'd be left out here alone. The glow from the sherry he'd nicked had been all too short-lived. His new jeans were soaked, his feet were freezing and his jacket leaked water down the back of his neck; he told himself he was shaking from the cold. But when the shouts rang out it was almost a relief.

"Stu? Come on, there's a good lad. We know you're out there. Don't make us come looking for you now - we'll send in the helicopter if we have to. Stu!"

He wrestled with himself. Could a chopper get off the ground in these conditions? He wouldn't have thought so, but what if he was wrong? The wilderness surrounded him, interminable, fogged with snow, and very, very cold. He could stay out here and freeze himself to death, or he could accept the inevitable arrest. It wasn't much of a contest when he thought about it. At least the cell that awaited him would be warm.

"Over here," he called, and waited for the burly figures to catch him up.

†††

Handcuffs in place, Stu subsided against the warm cloth seat of the police car and dripped. He could kick himself for dragging them into this with his loud mouth and his plans. They'd wasted the evening, lost all their loot, and now they'd miss Christmas banged up in the local nick. "I don't understand," he said, when his teeth had stopped chattering enough to get the words out. "Trish said... I mean, someone told me the police don't come out when it snows."

The constable driving the car had arrested Stu four times in the past and knew him well enough to know what he meant. "Well, that's a load of bollocks. The local gangs would have a free-for-all every time the roads were bad. We'd never be allowed to get away with that."

"Mind you, Dave," said his mate, "you'd be amazed how many buggers seem to think it's true. Year after year some idiot goes out and robs a place, and all we have to do is follow his footsteps in the snow."

Stu sat in his puddle of meltwater and scowled, not best pleased at the implication he was an idiot. Even if it was true, because he was the one who'd first believed Trish, who'd believed her friend Gail, who'd believed her old man. But one of them had got it wrong.

"So who was it phoned the cops?" he said at last. "We thought all the houses were empty but some bugger must have been hiding in the bath, and dialled 999 the minute we'd gone. For you to get there so fast, that is."

"Oh, no, it wasn't the householders who shopped you." Dave fought the steering - even his Land Rover was having problems on the wintry road. "It was your wife."

"Trish? Don't be daft. Trish wouldn't do a thing like that." But even as he said it, a nasty feeling trickled down his spine which had nothing to do with melting snow.

Sure enough, the second cop leered. "Expect she wanted

the night free, without her old man hanging round. She's been having it off with Brian from Traffic for months."

"You what? But... but I've been giving myself hell because I paid for that boob job when I couldn't afford it. That's why...." Too late he realised he was giving too much away. Then he shrugged. They'd probably already worked it out for themselves. "That's why we're out in this bloody weather in the first place."

The second cop sniggered. "You might want to have words with that wife of yours. She had that op for Brian's sake, because he likes his women nice and big. He's been boasting about it in the squad room for weeks - how he got some poor sap to pay while he reaped the rewards."

"Hey," Dave added. "It wasn't Brian who told you about the police not going out in the snow, was it? Looks like you've been had. Hook line and bloody sinker. And I'll bet he's having the last laugh." He glanced at his watch. "Right about... now."

Stu digested that one, which took him some time. His brain hurt, his legs hurt, his stomach hurt from the sherry and the chocolates and a generous slug of acid bile. That bastard Brian, shafting his wife and laughing at him all this time. Probably at it this very minute, now that Stu was safely out of the way. Wrapped round each other like an old pair of sheets, bonking like rabbits, Trish's new boobs thumping against his chest.

Or maybe not. Blue lights strobed the snow on the opposite side of the road, lighting up a scene from hell. Two cars with their sides stoved in and a third tipped on its roof. Police shuffled like penguins in a storm, setting up diversions and waving traffic through.

"That mate of yours Brian," he said, leaning across for a closer look. "He works Traffic, doesn't he? And you said the police always come out, even when it snows. So there's not much chance of him getting his leg over tonight. He's more likely to be out here, helping with this lot. Just think. He's out here, and I'll be banged up nice and snug in a cell all night, so there's no one around to keep Trish warm." He grinned, and the grin turned into a belly laugh. "Looks like I've got the last laugh after all."

Liverpool lass **Tess Makovesky** *is now settled in the far north of England where she roams the fells with a brolly, dreaming up new stories and startling the occasional sheep.*

Tess writes a distinctive brand of British comédie noir and her short stories have darkened the pages of various anthologies and magazines, including Shotgun Honey, Pulp Metal Magazine, Out of the Gutter Online, Betty Fedora, 'Exiles: An Outsider Anthology' (Blackwitch Press), 'Drag Noir' (Fox Spirit), 'Rogue' (Near to the Knuckle), and 'Locked and Loaded' (One Eye Press).

You can follow her ramblings (both literary and literal) at her blog: http://tessmakovesky.wordpress.com.

The Bitch Pit

Christopher Pimental

"To the war of love that no one ever wins. To the hues of Fall that never were. To the running leaves that burn so red, and to tragic heroes, who kill each other, battling enemies already dead."

PART I

No Way Out

I was a salesman; not a killer, but this was war.

There we were, marching underground through a sweltering tunnel, sucking dust and sweating clay-two midgets, the Texan and me-waiting for my chance to jam a shiv into the Texan's kidney, and get out clean.

I'd followed him to a sugar cane field in the dead of night, where the midgets were waiting in a dimly lit bamboo shack. Colombian rebels, they wore battle-scarred boots and black fatigues.

The bigger one had coarse black hair, and no front teeth.

At the moment, he was walking on lead. Thick for a runt, he was silent, rugged and mean. But he was a midget. Had no weapon, and walked with a limp. So if the shit hit the fan down here, I figured I could take him.

It was the second one though, a dwarf with Coke-bottle eyes and shoe-leather skin, that had my nuts in a bunch.

Me and the Texan had shared quite a chuckle when we first laid eyes on the myopic thing. No bigger than a chimp, he'd stomped at the dirt and yakked on and on about out not wanting to lead a pair of gringo pigs to the end of the line. Christ, old Tex nearly spit a lung laughing at those magnified eyes.

Now though, with the dwarf gimping behind us with a head full of steam-and his finger twitching on the trigger of a loaded AK-47-it didn't seem so goddamned funny.

Especially considering where we were headed.

Four paces ahead, the bigger midget continued his relentless pace, leading us beneath bulbs that poked out of the red clay tunnel at twenty-meter gaps, lighting just enough dust to see as far as the next murky bulb. From a distance came the muffled sound of pit bulls barking. And babies crying, which only added to the blood-beat already pounding in my ears.

The Texan didn't seem to mind though.

He was a salesman, too. A loudmouth with happy teeth and a smile so fake I could taste saccharine whenever he grinned. And he grinned a lot. Although at the moment he was struggling to keep pace, wiping sweat off his arms.

"You gonna make it?" I asked.

He wore leather sandals, tan cargo shorts as big as army

tents and a pink Polo shirt that was drenched under the pits. As he trudged along, he stooped his head and walked in a half-lean, half-simian motion to keep his forehead from smacking the light bulbs.

He took a breath and showed me those teeth. "Hell yeah, chief. I wouldn't miss this for the world."

I swallowed a mouthful of bile.

For the life of me, I couldn't figure out why a steak-fed guy like him wanted to visit the Bitch Pit, a place I'd heard of but hoped never to see. In this part of the world though, that was his problem. Not mine.

We were in Ecuador, a third-world banana regime whose peasant military was mired balls deep in a two-year war with Peru. Some dispute over an oil-rich stretch of jungle and blah, blah, blah.

Whatever.

All that mattered was each day soldiers were getting their asses blown off, eating bullets or catching diseases. That meant whore-loads of cash were just begging to be made if you knew the right people.

And, I knew the right people.

Starting with Raul Marin. The Minister of Public Health. A life-long politician and crooked as a Mick cop's smile. From day one of this skirmish, he'd guaranteed I was the only medical supplier authorized to bring in provisions for the war. And believe you me, the money was rolling in.

Our scam was simple. For five cents on the dollar, we

purchased expired antibiotics, I.Vs, pills-and whatever other crap I could jam into a shipping container-out of China. We smuggled it in country through Raul's back channels, re-labeled the dates and jacked the prices to thirty times cost before dumping it all on the front lines.

Easy as cream.

The only problem was it got to where we were bringing in so much expired gack that it began to pile up faster than our soldiers could get shot. That's when Raul devised a plan to sell the surplus to his counterpart in Peru. Blood money on the back end, lining our pockets with enough cash to live any man's dream. And, all of it bankrolled through a special contingency fund that Raul had set-up months before the war.

Of course, we had to spread a little cheese to make sure certain troublemakers in the government got their share. But that was business as usual in Ecuador. And no one cared.

Until the elections came around.

That's when these ignorant spics elected their new top banana-a jungle messiah who pledged to drag them out of misery and into the middle class. Little more than a thug dressed in a shiny black suit, his slick tongue and anti-corruption rhetoric brought him a landslide victory.

Now, emboldened by his fame, he was threatening to form a citizen's revolution. To change "business as usual", promising to prosecute every corrupt politician from the outgoing regime-which had our contacts fleeing the country with whatever cash they had.

Fact is I'd been ready to disappear, too. But Raul claimed he had a way to set things right. Keep the cash flowing. Even from within the new regime.

Doing the Texan was key to his plan.

†††

Twenty minutes into the trek, the tunnel opened to a small, dirt chamber, lit by a single yellow bulb. At the far end, two black doors loomed like passages to Hell.

As we approached, the lead midget signaled us to stop. He ticked a nod at his partner.

The dwarf waddled forward, and in his strongest helium balloon voice, ordered us to stand beside the doors. He positioned us with our backs to the clay then stood beside the bigger midget and leveled the AK-47 at our chests.

With blood zinging in my ears, I eyed the Texan, standing to my left. He was heaving at the shoulders, trying to catch his breath. Behind the doors, pit bulls barked and snarled, closer now. Bitches screamed, and babies cried. All of it coming through in waves.

I took a breath, eyed the barrel of that rifle, its cold, dead eye staring into my brain.

If that ugly dwarf decided to squeeze the trigger…Chirst, no one would hear us die.

Just as I was about to snap my knife out of my pocket and remind them we were Americans, and how they would be in a world of shit with the embassy if the dwarf shot us, the bigger midget gimped forward, his boot-heels scuffing the dirt. He stopped in front of the Texan.

"Escoge," he said.

The Texan eyed the midget. "What's that partner?"

"Escoge una puerta."

"I don't speak Es-pan-yol, son. Don't know what the hell you're saying." He grinned.

The midget hitched his thumbs into his waistband and took a step closer. "Escoge. Una. Puerta. Gringo de mierda. Los perros o las putas?"

The Texan smiled then looked at me and shrugged.

"He wants you to choose a door," I said. "The one with the dogs or the one with the whores." My fingers released the pocketknife.

The Texan showed me his teeth. "Hell, partner. Why didn't you tell me?" He eyed the midget again, clapped his hands together and said, "I'll take whatever door has them pootahs."

The midget nodded, his mouth slithering into a toothless grin. The Texan grinned right back. Even the dwarf smiled.

Fucking cheers all around.

Except from me.

The new president was to be sworn-in this coming Thursday at 12:00 p.m.

Eliminating the Texan before then was key to Raul's plan.

Raul had minions-quiet, heartless men whose business it was to make people disappear. Entire families had vanished in the dead of night at Raul's behest, only to turn up days later in bits and pieces in some mango grove or swamp.

The Texan was my responsibility, he'd said. To show that I was still committed. That we were partners till the end of this little war.

I'd been tailing the Texan for three days. Till now, the tunnel had been my only chance to get close enough to do him. But that dwarf had been waddling behind us every inch of the way. And now, somewhere beyond those doors, a crowd full of witnesses waited.

If I didn't find a way to get it done, how long before Raul's men would be coming after me?

The Texan chose the door to the right.

The lead midget keyed it open and we followed him into another dimly lit tunnel, this one descending into the earth on a subtle downward slope. The smell of blood and feces hung in the air like the stench of a black market pet store. The deeper we descended, the stronger it grew.

So did the ruckus from the dogs.

And of course, those goddamned babies continued to scream.

Soon, the tunnel veered left, snaked another fifty meters in and then opened to a chamber of sorts. And what I saw to either side caused my head to spin.

To the right, steel dog cages, caked with rust and stacked three-high, stood side-by-side against the crumbling clay. Filthy pit bulls paced and snarled inside each, slamming their snouts against the bars as we approached.

Someone had positioned the female dogs between the males' cages. It was clear from the coppery stench that some of the bitches were in heat-their vulvae sagging between their legs, swollen and leaking like blood-wet papayas-which heightened the males' aggression, making them dick-wild for any battles to come.

Each time one of the hormone-crazed dogs snapped its jaws, my stomach clenched at the thought of how easily those teeth would cut through flesh and shatter bone.

Bad as that was though, the dirty Hispanic females locked in cages to my left, naked and panting, stopped me. They moaned as I passed. Some hunched on all fours, others lying on their sides, hugging their knees, cramped inside their filthy prisons, the stench of piss and shit simmering from within. On top of each cage, handwritten cardboard signs identified whether they were from Ecuador or Peru.

Most of the women wore dirt caked on their skin, their hair, and under their nails. All of them were injured or bleeding. One had her ear partially torn, dangling and smeared to her cheek like bloody Silly Putty.

Her cardboard sign indicated she was from Peru.

As I approached, she clawed at her cage, her gnarled fingers scraping the metal bars. Other women pleaded around me too, reaching out with their hands, begging in Spanish-por favor por favor-to save their babies.

Christ, their babies. Infants. Dozens of them. Screaming. Penned inside modified animal traps that had been positioned in front of their mothers, just out of reach.

The babies were naked, too, and desperate with rash, crammed and twisted within barely adequate space. No blankets. No booties. No mother's milk. Just animals. Wailing in perfect discord.

All of it pressing in on me.

As I advanced, struggling to breathe, the Texan caught up and threw his arm over my shoulder.

"Ain't this something, partner?" he said.

"What?" I said, wriggling free of his arm.

"I said ain't this something? You ever seen anything like

it?" He walked wide-eyed, breathing through his teeth.

Bile burned at the back of my throat "Sure. Partner," my hand wandering into my pocket.

The Texan slapped my back and advanced, his head swiveling from side to side, like a tourist on a sightseeing trek. I slowed my pace, curled my fingers around the knife and threw a cautious glance over my shoulder.

The dwarfling had stopped behind us. He was sneering in front an infant's cage, one of the few babies that was calm. Bending at the waist, the dwarf snorted and spit between the tiny bars, spattering the infant's cheeks with a gob of yellow phlegm.

The baby mewled.

The dwarf sneered and then raised the butt of his rifle and slammed it down onto the metal trap, rattling the infant to the bones. When the baby shrieked, the dwarf spit at him again and then waddled toward the next one in line.

As he advanced, our eyes met. He lifted the rifle, dared me with his gaze. I turned away, my head still spinning.

Behind me, he spit again, and smashed another cage.

Another baby screamed.

When the dwarfling laughed again, my face grew hot. The knife was in my hand before I knew it. I turned and rushed him; planning to smash the blade through his Coke-bottle eyes, stab him over and over until his sockets gushed with blood. When I was within distance, I raised my arm, and was about to hammer it down, when the Texan appeared out of nowhere. He grabbed my wrist and yanked me backwards.

"Easy there partner," he said, his grip like a wrench.

I blinked up at him, air seething in and out of me.

He ticked a nod at the knife. "Put that fool thing away. We don't need no trouble down here. Not in this part of the world."

I looked into his eyes, and then at the tiny blade.

Behind us, the dwarf advanced to another cage, the rifle firm in his stubby clutch. I gripped the knife, eying the Texan hard, Raul's orders urging me to attack. But, the man had just saved my life. And the dwarf was near.

I sighed.

"That's it. Take a breath," the Texan said and eyed the dwarf over my shoulder before releasing his grip. "That dwarf back there, ain't nothing but a thing."

With Raul screaming in my head, I cautiously pocketed the knife.

The Texan urged me forward. "This is war, partner." He waved his hand at the women and the babies. "None of this matters. But I know how you feel. I was like you the first time, too."

His words stopped me. "Wait. You've been here before?"

He threw his head back and laughed. "Buddy, this is my fourth trip down here. Got me a dog in play this time, too. A Peruvian gal they snagged in one of their free diaper-and-milk scams. Rosa something-or-other. Squeezed her first kid out two months ago. Just enough time for her to get attached." He winked. "Should be a real brawl."

The tunnel began to spin.

Somewhere behind me, the dwarf advanced.

Another baby shrieked.

The Texan threw his arm over my shoulder again. "Let's giddy 'up, partner. Don't wanna be late." He tossed another glance over his shoulder and led me past the bleeding women. Their infants. And the dogs.

All of it coming as if from a distance now.

The fact is, I'd heard of the Bitch Pit. How, during the war, events had escalated beyond just dogfights. The mothers. Their babies. The horror of it all. But, I'd never really believed.

Now though, walking the last few yards of the tunnel in a haze, the full weight of where we were going finally bore down on me, heavy as the Texan's arm around my neck.

So heavy I couldn't find the strength to wriggle free.

When we finally exited the cavern and caught up to the midget on point, he led us down a final path toward a dirt archway that was covered by a black plastic tarp. Above the entrance, a hand-written cardboard sign read: ENTRADA V.I.P.

Crowd noise roared from the other side. A hive buzzing with taunts, shouts, and jeers. Pit bulls barked and growled. Women shrieked. The babies screamed.

When the midget directed us to approach, I eyed that sign again-VIP ENTRANCE-and almost laughed.

But then the midget parted the curtain...and led us in.

PART 2

Hell

The crowd was raucous, packed into the steaming arena like flies. Hundreds of them. Unwashed, third world peasants-who, by their stench, used neither deodorant nor toilet paper-standing twenty deep, jockeying for a view around a forty-foot rectangular pit.

The Texan had elbowed his way to the front of the crowd and positioned himself beside the lead midget at the edge. A thin rope ran the length of the pit's perimeter, the only barrier against a twelve-foot drop over the brink, where thirty pit bulls ran in packs, snapping their jaws.

As a tall, white Gringo, the Texan drew whistles and catcalls from the rabble behind him. He was oblivious though. Already mesmerized by the spectacle of the night's first battle.

The set-up was simple but hard: two women, fighting naked in a cage the size of an elevator car, which was set atop 15-foot mound of dirt, dead center of the pit.

Six feet above the cage, a thick, wooden beam jutted from the clay. Pulley rigs were bolted at opposite ends of the lumber. Hemp rope hung from either side. Screaming infants dangled from the bottom of each rope, tied at the ankles like bait.

While their mothers battled, soldiers splashed the babies with cupfuls of blood, sending the crowd into frenzy. Of course, at the bottom of the ditch, the pit bulls yammered too, climbing all over each other as they attempted to scale the dirt to get at the dripping newborns.

Taking it all in, I stood behind the Texan, my stomach in a knot, the rabble in the crowd jostling me from side to side, rubbing up on me with their hot, wet skin.

Within moments the first battle ended when an

Ecuadorean mother collapsed in the cage. The crowd roared, the Texan's fist pumping leading the way. When a sneering soldier cut one of the infants free and dangled it like meat above the howling dogs, the crowd surged, clamoring as he tossed the baby in.

The pit bulls charged as a pack, and tore into the child.

Mercifully, its mother, beaten unconscious by her Peruvian rival, never saw the carnage.

I saw it though.

And, I saw the Texan cheer.

As the night grew old and the crowd swarmed to fever pitch, the Texan defended his front row perch with belligerence and size, eagerly waiting for his dog to take center stage.

Fight after fight, he howled and leered as each pair of captive, Hispanic women battled naked in the cage-scratching, biting, and bashing each other's head into the bars-in an attempt to save their children.

In his Gringo-Spanish, the Texan urged the soldiers to slather the mothers' "brown bastards" red with blood, which riled the masses even more.

Through it all, I stood behind him in a haze, forcing my eyes to see. To view the carnage and to watch the Texan as he cheered and placed bets on death.

This was war, he'd said. None of it mattered. Nothing but a thing.

Another fight ended. A soldier dangled the losing mother's infant twins above the pit. The Texan high-fived the midget to his left and turned to me with a grin on his face and a hard-on bulging in his shorts.

"We just made twenty bucks!" he said.

Nothing but a thing.

He turned back just as the soldier tossed the baby girls to the dogs.

As the Texan leaned over the rope to get a birds-eye view of the slaughter, the crowd behind him heaved forward.

My head reeling, I could watch no more. I shifted with the surge and planted my right hand on the Texan's hip. And shoved.

The Texan flailed. Tried to compensate. Then, the rope snapped under his weight.

His name was Arnold Cook, 49. A pharmaceutical distributor out of Dallas, and the new president's handpicked partner in crime.

It had taken Raul's minions a month to identify him, and another week to locate him in country. And according to their sources, the new, anti-corruption president would take a 75% cut of everything the Texan brought in to support the war.

When the Texan tumbled into the pit, the crowd surged again en masse, roaring as the dogs converged. I watched long enough to see a white bitch tear out his throat.

Then I backpedaled and pushed through the crowd, throwing constant looks behind me until I made it through the plastic curtain and into the tunnel, breathless.

It was only when I approached the human zoo did my feet finally slow. There, I waited in the shadows off the entryway with my knife poised and my back pressed to the clay, listening for the lead midget's footsteps, sure he'd figured out what I'd done.

In the distance behind me, the crowd roared. The dogs howled and babies screamed. In the cavern to my left, women rattled in their cages.

I waited until it became clear that no one had cared. Not even the midget emerged. What did it matter? He'd already been paid.

My breath slowing, I stepped out of the shadows, stole a glance to either side and set my thoughts on the cavern. All I had to do was walk the gauntlet. Ignore the babies and their mothers without losing my mind, and I would be halfway home.

I would have done it too, if I hadn't stepped into the cavern and seen the dwarfling hunched on all fours, rattling one of the baby cages. He was barking and snarling at the hysterical infant like a pit bull. His rifle lay on the dirt beside him.

While the kid shrieked in its cage, its Peruvian mother pleaded with the dwarf to stop. He spit at her in response, and then spit at her kid.

By time he saw me lurch forward, it was already too late.

He reached for the rifle, but I kicked him in the jaw. He smacked face-first against the cage then, groaning, rolled over on the dirt, scrambling for the A.K.

I sneered, let him get close and then stomped on his hand, the satisfying crunch of bones beneath my boot. The tiny grunt howled. Behind me, the dogs exploded in frenzy, slamming their snouts against their cages. The Latinas rustled with life, watching from their pens as my body heat swelled.

I stood over the dwarf, arms trembling, preparing to stomp.

He scuttled backward, cradling his hand to his chest like a wounded bird.

"Por favor. Por favor," he gibbered, pleading with those myopic, Coke-bottle eyes.

I laughed in response. Raised my foot and kicked that hand again. He screed and shuffled backward just as the Peruvian mother reached through her cage. She clawed a handful of the dwarfling's hair and yanked, slamming his skull to the metal bars. Then she snaked her right arm around his throat and sank home a chokehold.

The dwarf kicked at the dirt.

The mother pulled and squeezed, pressing against the cage until one of her mocha colored breasts popped through the bars.

The midget gurgled. Veins as thick as tree grubs swelled on his forehead. His peasant skin darkened to a purple-maroon, his eyes bulging like a tree frog's behind those lenses.

The mother strangled him until it seemed the dwarf's eyes would burst in a spray of black and red, but then, the bastard clamped onto the her pinky finger. He wrenched it from his throat, twisted and then bent until it snapped.

The Latina screed. Lost her grip.

The dwarf flopped to the dirt, struggled for breath and then, in a fit of rage, kicked her baby's cage, sending it tumbling over the clay. The infant screamed. It's mother hissed. The dwarf scrambled for his rifle.

Shocked out of my stupor, I lunged forward and in a singular, predatory motion, dropped to a knee and hammer-plunged my knife into the dwarf's ribcage. The dwarf stiffened with a gasp, gurgling for breath and pawing at the blade. I slapped his hand away, tried to yank the knife out, but it was sunk too deep, caught under bone. So I stood, smiled at the writhing bastard then stomped on the hilt, driving it all the way home.

The dwarf's legs shot forward, his eyes rolling to their whites. While he struggled for air, blood seeped through his drab uniform in an expanding crimson stain around the hilt. In agony, he made grunting noises like a garfish out of water, blood bubbling to his lips.

Still, the little monkey refused to die.

With the babies and dogs going insane, I clutched the dwarf by his ankles and hoisted him off the ground.

No heavier than a chimp, he wriggled in my clutch, trying to kick out and jerk free. I held fast though, and swung him around and around by his ankles. When I finally got up to speed, I stepped forward and banged his head against the Peruvian mother's cage. His temple exploded. He went limp in my hands.

Dizzy, and with the Latina women watching in shock, I slung him to the ground. He landed in a face-up heap, his mouth contorted in a snarl. Somehow, those glasses, held by a strap, had remained in place. Behind one Coke-bottle lens, he stared out at me through a dead, magnified eye.

With the dogs snarling, I lifted the dwarf's warm body and hurled it behind one of their filthy cages.

Then I stood there for a time, trying to catch my breath.

From her cage, the Peruvian mother caught me with her eyes. We shared an awkward glance, and then she pointed at her baby.

I approached its toppled cage, righted it and pushed it

closer to hers. Then, I retrieved the dwarf's AK-47 and slipped it through her metal bars.

I refused to look back after that. Just lowered my gaze and raced out into the tunnel. The rest of the Hispanic women reached through their cages as I passed, pleading with me again to save their babies. But I just kept moving forward. I was a salesman, not a hero... and those bitches were someone else's war.

Christopher Pimental *was born in Massachusetts. A former international investigator, he has firsthand knowledge of the gritty side of the streets. And of the terrible things people do to each other. After many years working undercover, he now consults and teaches in a private university.*

The Shark Cage

Gareth Spark

Flynn lit a cigarette, looked at the boat and then walked back to the car. Charlie leaned over, unlocked the door. His long white hair hung loose around his collar. 'So?'

'Don't like it.'

'I'm telling you, Morisette's there.'

'Then why won't he answer his phone?'

'Maybe he turned it off.'

'I heard it ringing.'

'He's a deaf old fuck,' Charlie said. 'My back is aching, let's get the gear and fuck off.'

'Something's not right.'

'You aren't a squaddie no more, boy; there isn't Taliban hiding round every fucking rock.'

Charlie opened the door and climbed out. The night was cool and the Mediterranean was a dim blue line beneath a sky like spilled petrol. 'You ignored me and brought it, didn't you?' He said as Flynn passed him.

'Of course I brought it.'

'If they catch you with a shooter…'

'They won't.' Flynn nodded at the boat; the name was dark against the white hull: Verge del Cami. He touched the grip of a Serbian 9mm pistol jammed into a concealed holster in the waistband of his jeans. 'I got a bad feeling.'

'Stay here if you want.' Charlie squeezed between cables running along the deck, moving sideways. 'I've got shit to do.'

He stood up on the boat, which moved slightly with the waves, and shouted, 'Hey!'

Flynn heard a heavy wood hatch slide across one of the companionways, then Charlie complaining at the lack of space, and then, 'Flynn!'

'What?'

'He's fucking dead.'

Flynn drew the weapon, thumbed the safety and ran to the boat. Charlie grabbed the shoulder of his coat and pulled him up. 'You got the gun, you go first.'

'Where is he?'

'To the left.' Charlie was breathless and his voice was high and frayed. 'The door blew open…in the wind…or I wouldn't have seen the fucker.'

'Shit'

Flynn inched his way inside. He heard nothing but the boat: creaking timber, loose cables, heavy water pushing the hull. Cheap panels lined the small corridor, reflecting the harsh white of a single bulb. A door flapped open to his left and closed again, slowly. It felt like the meat aisle of a supermarket, the same chill and perfume of old blood. Flynn moved forward, listened, and then tapped the door open all the way with his toe. His throat was like sandpaper. There was a tiny shower cubicle in the corner of the square room.

He pulled a cord for the light, heart thumping so fast it hurt.

Morisette's body was slumped forward, hands fastened by plasticuffs to a towel rail. The edges of the ties cut deeply into his wrists and blood pooled beneath him, glistening and dark. A stained white robe lay loose around his body. 'Jesus Christ.'

'I told you.' It was Charlie. He stood in the doorway and pointed at the body as though Flynn might have missed it.

'Don't touch anything,' the latter said, trying to be calm, professional. 'Where did Sean say the gear was?'

'In the lifebelts.'

Flynn reached over, killed the light and pulled the door shut. He saw bloody footprints leading away. 'Get 'em,' he said. 'Take 'em back to the car, ring Sean.'

'What are you gonna do?'

He gestured with the pistol towards the footprints and glanced at Charlie. 'Go on then.'

Charlie turned and tripped over the steps. Flynn sighed. The end of the corridor was dark and he waited for his eyes to adjust, watching for movement. He tried the handles of the doors between the bathroom and the end of the hall. The last door was open. He peered around the corner; it was the main cabin. A brass wheel shone faintly in the darkness, and he saw the open sea through broad windows. He patted the wall, found a switch and flicked it, filling the room with a warm light flooding up from smoked glass sconces. The wheelhouse was chaotic: charts lay across the instrument panel; cupboards left open; even the first aid kit had been broken open, contents scattered. He moved into the room, weapon raised and felt a sharp cold across his face. Doors, to his right, open, leading out to the deck and in the same moment he realised where the men were, he heard Charlie shout his name.

Flynn turned and ran back. He slipped in one of the larger bloody footprints and fell to his knees with a curse. There was a sudden high-pitched cry. Flynn stood, tried to control his breathing, and rushed into the night.

He saw one of them straight away: shaved head; bomber jacket; blue jeans, standing on the gangway with the lifebelts over his shoulder. He stared at Flynn with a bored expression. The other man had Charlie. He pushed a sawed-off shotgun tight against the old man's jaw. Dark electricity crackled in his eyes. Flynn switched his aim from one man to the other. Neither displayed alarm. Flynn's pulse thumped heavily. The man on the gangway said something in a language Flynn could not place, addressing his comrade. He looked tired and there were brown bloodstains across the front of his jeans. Tattooed spiders covered his hands, from the wrists to the fingers.

The other man replied without taking his eyes from Flynn. Tattoos, carrying the lifebelts, walked down to the jetty.

Flynn watched him go. The back of his throat burned and he said to the man holding Charlie. 'I don't know who you are but that gear's ours, bought and paid for. Let him go, bring it back, maybe we can sort this.' His finger lay loose against the trigger. Charlie stared at him. He seemed to struggle for breath.

The man shook his head slowly. A scar ran up his cheek and across his left eye, which was dull, probably glass, Flynn noted. There was noise behind him, boots, starting slow, rushing through the vessel, then a blinding flash, and then he knew nothing.

Flynn came round sluggishly and glanced at his watch. He'd been out a quarter of an hour. Still alive, he thought, hurting too much to be dead. Blood ran from his scalp where the blow had landed and he staunched the flow with a bandana dug out of his pocket. The air stank of blood and salt and he crawled across to Charlie, who lay across a pool of standing water. Flynn was dizzy, nauseated by the blow. 'Charlie?' He shook the old man's foot and pulled himself upright. Charlie had taken both barrels to the face. Blood ran across the deck. They were setting him up. He glanced around, searching for the flash of blue that would presage the arrival of the Mossos d'Esquadra, Catalunya's Police force; he hadn't much time.

He took the keys from Charlie's pocket and ran to the car…

Three nights later and Flynn drove quickly along the road from Sant Carles to Pineda. Bars and restaurants ran along the left while to the right, pale sand stretched into the darkness of the sea. There were no stars, just the sensation of being beneath something, as though a vast screen had closed across the sky, trapping the heat and menaces, making the air boil. He felt a thick tear of sweat run across the corner of his brow and lifted a hand from the slick steering wheel to wipe it away.

He passed a crumbling sandstone tower that stood above Esquirol beach and then lost sight of the sand behind rows of large square hotels and apartment blocks. He turned left and passed a church half-hidden behind a screen of pines, crossed a rail bridge and spun the struggling jeep onto a steep bank that was deep with dust. The house was at the top of the hill, behind a tall fence that circled the property. Flynn killed the engine and sat. The vehicle stunk of heated plastic and old cigarettes and he stepped out after a while and walked across to the sun-bleached gates twice his height. The gravel crunched beneath his feet like spilled breakfast cereal. He reached the recessed steel plate of the intercom and pressed the button. 'Yeah?' Sean's voice scratched from the tiny speaker.

'It's me.'

'So it is.'

There was a click and the gates began to open. Flynn climbed back in the car and drove into the compound. Sean's chunky silhouette loomed in the open doorway of the house. Doric columns framed the door. The big man waved a spade-like hand in salute as Flynn parked, climbed from the car and crossed the yard. 'Well, here he is,' Sean said, the words mangled by a gruff, south London accent the years and distance had never tamed. 'Short sleeves an' all, you know, the night breeze can kill a man.'

'A lot of things can.'

Sean was a broad man with thinning hair, a shaggy goatee, and small, vindictive eyes 'How are things at the bar?'

'I didn't think you'd give a damn.'

'I need to take an interest in my legit businesses, to know

what's what, in case the cops ever ask.'

'Business is fine.'

Sean ushered him inside, then slammed the door and waddled across the floor in bare feet, leaving a trail of moist footprints.

'Where's Carmen?' Flynn asked, getting straight to the point. 'You didn't tell me she was going away.'

'She's just gone, leave it at that.' Sean spoke with an odd, tight voice, walking ahead of Flynn into the living room: leather sofas, a bar of rough stone and cement, tropical fish tank in the corner and deep cream carpets. 'I got the farm. Whiskey?'

'That would do the trick. I could find her if you like.'

Sean poured the drinks in silence and then said. 'Let's talk about something else.'

'You said something about the farm?'

'Already had it knocked to the ground and the new build is up. Carmen said to call it Casa d'Esclaus. Don't know what it means, but it's got a ring to it.' He frowned and sipped from the drink, hovering behind the bar like a waiter at the point of quitting. 'Had to borrow a bit more from London's money, but we don't need to worry about that, not when you get the gear back. Charlie cost me more than I care to say. Wish I'd shut my ears when he come in with his brilliant idea, fucking coke and his old fucking contacts, serves me right for being greedy.'

'Haven't Carmen's family lived on that farm forever?'

'There are no more forevers.'

'You think it was Charlie then? Maybe said the wrong thing to the wrong man?'

'I knew Charlie most of my life, and he was a real black hat back in the day, but these last few years, he'd gone soft; wasn't careful enough.'

'We three were the only ones who knew anything about it, other than the Morrisette, but he had no idea what was onboard.' Flynn sat on the nearest sofa and stroked his jaw where the new beard itched. 'That leaves the brothers.'

'It was one of our lads.'

'You know that for a fact.'

'I finally got hold of Charlie's mates who sold him the coke. They heard about the drama and the lot of them went into hiding. They told me. Morrisette, for some reason he took to the grave, thought it best to take someone down with him. That's who set all this up.'

'Then we need to find the fucker.'

'This gangbang's cost us.' He leaned forward on the bar. 'Flynn, the Stelescus put up half a million Euro for this and I have had to pay them with the money from London because Cezar Stelescu is here and they're over the water. Priorities, you see. I did what I had to.' He rubbed his eyes and said. 'You need to find that coke.'

'I will.'

'That's what I like to hear.'

'We might have trouble with Roy Quinn too. He was in the bar last night, made a nuisance of himself.' Flynn sipped from his drink. 'Smashed a few things, grabbed one of the girls, beat up the guy on the door.'

'He's a little bastard,' Sean said. 'I know I'm his godfather and it was my idea to bring him over, give him some work, but he's a burden I could do without. Thinks he's in a Guy

Ritchie film. He's causing trouble because he sees the way you run things down here and wishes it was him. He wants that respect.'

'Then he's got a lot coming to him. The way he drops names, you'd think he was something more than a second rate fighter that couldn't stay on his feet. He was with Marku Stelescu. They're always together.'

Sean wiped his forehead with a blue handkerchief. 'They're a lot alike, I suppose. Just watch him. I don't want him causing trouble, not now. In a few months, we won't have to care about any of them, London, Stelescus, no-one.' He laid a hand on Flynn's shoulder. 'Meantime there's something I want you to do for me, take a delivery to the Casa d'Esclaus, something coming over the border; can't trust anyone else to do it. An old truck carrying the shit Cezar wants at the farm. I want you to collect it.'

Flynn felt the muscles tighten across his face; a feeling, nothing good. 'When?'

'Tomorrow night. You meet them outside Piera, the usual place. Take Roy with you.'

'If anything goes wrong this time we'll end up like Charlie. Cezar won't fuck around.'

Sean turned away and scratched at the leather surface of the desk with a thumbnail as he spoke. 'I lost a lot of money.' He coughed again. 'And didn't quite have enough to pay 'em what they lost on that boat. I need to let them peddle some shit outta the farm.'

'I wouldn't trust 'em too much'.

The sky was black when Flynn left. He gazed down from the hill as he walked to the parked jeep. There was glow like a distant battle in the sky above Pineda, and always the faint tremble of traffic and the sea. Roy Quinn, he thought, twenty-five years old and he thinks he knows everything; he had taken money from a trio of professional gamblers during his time in the ring and hadn't gone down as intended. He would be dead if Sean hadn't asked the Firm for a favour. That was three men's lives around Roy's neck, not that he cared. Flynn heard him, one night, telling the story to the other doormen, making out that he was too cunning, too dangerous, not built for defeat. Flynn knew how easily it could have gone another way.

It made him miss Charlie even more. Charlie Hartigan was of the old school; started out running errands for a mob south of the river. He and Sean worked their way up through the Firm until a bad decision cost them the reputation that was everything. People were hurt and Jack O'Brian, the big man, sent the three of them into exile, set them up so they could launder London's dirty money through the bar and club. Then Charlie chanced across an old friend in Marbella on the run since the 80's who'd gone into smuggling in a big way, the Stelescus appeared, and Flynn watched as Charlie and Sean began to forget they had masters in London .

He climbed into the jeep and waited a moment as the gates opened before him and wondered if it would ever end, if there would be a day when he was not completely afraid. Only when you are in the ground, he thought, and that might be sooner rather than later.

†††

Night had come swiftly from the hills. It was cold, and Flynn turned up the collar of his jacket. A car's horn blared from the corner and Flynn waved for the driver to keep quiet. It was a dark blue Mercedes, parked on the kerb. Roy reached across and flicked the lock down on the passenger door and Flynn climbed in, puffing a little as he fought with the seatbelt. He turned to Roy and asked, 'You got it then?'

The young man had a nervous smile as he handed over a heavy, oil-stained paper bag from which Flynn drew a handgun. Flynn held the weapon in the palm of his hand. It was a small, short-recoil 9mm pistol, numbers ground off; same as the one he'd lost the night Charlie was killed. 'You haven't got the safety on,' Flynn said, pulling back the top slide and checking there was a round in the chamber before thumbing down the catch.

'Yeah, well, I don't know anything 'bout guns, do I?' Roy bit his thumbnail and glanced at the weapon, then at the door, as though preparing to run. 'What's all this about anyway?'

'Hasn't your friend Marku told you?'

'Ain't seen him.'

'We're going for a ride, nothing more. You got the rest?'

Roy reached into the breast pocket of his shirt and handed him the spare clip. 'Why you need the gun then?'

'Nervous are we?'

'No.'

'Then calm the fuck down. You're driving me to Piera, nothing else. We can have a chat on the way.'

'I can't help it,' Roy said, 'being jumpy. I get that way

sometimes.'

'Too much shit in your system,' Flynn said. 'Let's go.'

Light washed across the bonnet of the car as Roy waited
for a gap in the traffic; Flynn watched it play over the beaten
smooth surface and emptied his mind of everything but that
light. Then it was gone.

†††

Piera, close to the French border, was small and pale in the
distance beneath the warm light of the moon. Flynn raised
a pair of supermarket binoculars, looked at the miniature
citadel of the town on its peak, and wondered what it offered:
a bar, certainly, probably nothing more. The Stelescus were
ten minutes late, but he couldn't discount the possibility that
they, like he, were watching cautiously from some concealed
position. Nobody trusted anybody. There was a rattle in the
dry bushes behind and he heard Roy swear. 'Keep it down,'
Flynn said.

'I don't know why we're hiding up here.'

'Don't want to take a chance after last time.'

'That was different.'

'Was it?' Flynn turned and looked at Roy for a long time,
then said, 'Not so different.' He reached round for the pistol
and checked the chamber again. He wanted Roy to see the
weapon, to remind him it was there.

The latter stared unhappily. 'I don't get it.'

'I'm just saying, it wasn't so different,' Flynn said. 'You were
there that night too.'

'Where'd you get that from? I fuckin' never heard a...'

'Shut up,' Flynn snapped. 'All I care about is finding that coke.' He lied easily. 'I know it was you Charlie sent down there. Now, why would he do a thing like that?'

Roy looked down, and after a while he said, 'I can't say.'

'All I want is the truth, Roy, and you can walk away from this.'

A voice rang out in the darkness and then a van drove slowly out of the barn, the engine hardly a throb in the night. It was a dark blue Ford Luton, moving at a creeping pace along the track. Men walked at either side of the track. Flynn turned the binoculars onto the roofless buildings and saw two dark 4x4s in front of the main house. He wiped the sweat from his eyes. Roy had vanished.

Flynn swore, then stood and started to descend the hill. His feet dragged in the dust as though trying to hold him back and his heart thumped heavily at the base of his throat. He walked towards the footbridge and crossed it with a carelessness that did not come easily; insects clicked in the reeds on the riverbanks and the light of the moon broke across the water. The pines were tall and stark against the warm sky and swayed a little in the breeze that Flynn could no longer feel. The weight of the pistol pulled against his belt at the back and he walked with his right hand free and ready to draw the weapon.

The other men had spread out across the dusty circle of the earth so as not to present too easy a target. They watched him impassively.

The van door opened and a high, amiable voice called: 'Flynn, my friend, come here why don't you. You kept us waiting for so long thought you were never going to come down from your hill.'

Flynn walked over quickly; a little more relaxed now he had heard that voice, as Marku Stelescu would not be there in person if the plan had changed. The Romanian sat in the van with the door open, smoking a cigarette, drumming his fingers on the wheel, grinning. Marku was a young 32, with long greasy hair pulled back into a ponytail. He wore a red hooded top, jeans and white trainers, and his small wrinkled eyes shone with a kind of manic energy. He spoke with head tipped back so that he looked down the length of his nose at Flynn. 'Did you hear they gave Marius and Tudor eighteen years each in Tarragona this morning?' He asked. 'He was always trying to act so tough, that putoi Marius, but still, that's a fuck of a long time to stare at your feet.'

'There's an old saying,' Flynn remarked. 'If you can't do the time, don't do the crime.'

Marku laughed a short bark that showed all his teeth. 'This is true,' he said, 'and can you do the time?'

'Already have and I don't want to do any more, so can we hurry it up?'

'Don't you want to know what is in the back?' Marku asked, gesturing with his thumb towards the box on the vehicle. There was some noise coming from it, but Flynn could not make it out above the rattle of the idling engine.'

'No.'

'You aren't curious?'

'No.'

Marku studied the other man for what seemed an age. The breeze lifted white powder in spirals from the road and it fell rattling against the side of the van. 'Good,' he said finally.

He flicked his cigarette out into the dust and said something in Romanian to the other men who, wordlessly, turned and began to walk back to the farm. 'Overkill,' Marku continued, 'but I need these men when I collect this van in Marseilles and especially when we come over the hills; that son of a bitch Petru Comarnescu, you know him?'

'No,' Flynn said.

He sold this tomberon to us and I have never trusted him. He's not straight like Sean and there always the chance I have to kill this man,' he said. 'Not this time maybe.'

'What does that word mean?'

'Word?'

'He sold us this what?'

'Oh!' Marku laughed and stepped down from the van. 'It is a little joke word of mine, it means for throwing your garbage into.'

'A bin?'

'This is the word.' He stepped out and handed Flynn a key on a yellow plastic fob. 'This opens the lock on the shutter in the back,' he said. 'My advice, for what it's worth, is driving steady, take the quiet roads. We go there now to meet you.'

'What if they stop me?'

Marku looked up at the sky and began to walk back to the farm. 'It is a beautiful night,' he said, 'just as you say, and this is a fine place.' He turned and smiled. 'Nobody knows what happened to the man who owned this house, do you know that?' He walked away, the heels of his boots stabbing into the ground.

Flynn puzzled over this statement before he decided it was some kind of threat; he'd be surprised if it wasn't. He climbed into the van and adjusted the seat to accommodate his longer legs. Bollocks, Flynn thought, they don't trust me if they trust anyone, not after what happened with Charlie; it cost them, and it'll take more than me driving this van for them to trust us.

The van was old and moved sluggishly out of the hills of Piera towards the main roads. The country was spectral in the light; he looked at his watch, it was half past twelve. The Romanians had wanted to meet, perhaps for some theatrical reason, at the stroke of midnight. There was a thud from the back of the van as something fell over in there and Flynn hoped it was nothing fragile.

Flynn drove for the next few hours, down through the high country towards the coastal plain; the mountains were tall and dark blue against the stars and the roads were quiet. He passed through several towns, each larger than the last, and stopped for petrol once before reaching Peratallada, which was the last town before the plain. The farm Sean had inherited, through his marriage to Carmen, stood twelve miles to the west.

Flynn lit a cigarette and waved the smoke away from his face. He turned the van down a straight road lined by broken walls; thorny trees seemed to grow in an arch across it and there were olive groves to one side; the moon had sunk. Flynn rubbed his eyes trying to see ahead through his fatigue. He pulled over to look at a map, and did not see the car driving towards him until it was a few yards away. Cops. He swore lightly as the young driver got out. The uniform was tight on him and he held the pistol at his hip as he walked, very slowly, to Flynn's window. Flynn leaned forward, pulled the ashtray from the dashboard and stubbed out the cigarette. He closed his eyes, opened them, prepared a smile and turned to the window. The police officer looked in, standing away from the window. The peak of his cap concealed his face and he spoke in quick Spanish.

Maintaining his smile, Flynn asked, 'Speak English?'

The young man spoke haltingly. 'What is wrong?' His accent was heavy and Flynn had the sense that he only knew the words as sounds. There was something familiar about him.

A breeze came through the window and cooled Flynn's forehead and he knew then how nervous he was as the sweat cooled. His arms tingled and thick blood pumped in his ears. 'I'm lost,' he said, 'trying to get to the' -he pretended to think- 'N-340; I want to get to the coast, got some things to deliver to a hotel I work for; there's a note somewhere.' He was careful to speak fast, hoping the young Spaniard would decide he had neither time nor energy for a long and difficult conversation.

The police officer leaned back and looked along the side of the van. 'What are you carrying?' He spoke with a more assured fluency this time and Flynn sensed something in the voice. The man stepped forward and stroked his fingers along the side of the truck and Flynn saw the tattoo of a spider on the back of his hand. He turned and stared at the car ahead. It was a plain white 4x4 of some kind: no lights, no paint job, no Guardia Civil, or Policia. 'Fruit machines,' he said. 'Your English is pretty good.'

'One must.'

'So what are we doing?'

'Would you mind stepping out of the cab, sir?'

The wind crept through the branches of the twisted trees and Flynn looked up as he asked, 'Is something wrong?'

'If you could just step out.'

The man was still smiling, but Flynn had noticed now that he wore no name badge and that his hand had not left the grip of his Star service pistol. He was calm suddenly and returned the smile. 'All right then.' He pushed the door and stepped out, planning, feeling the dread cold all the way through him now. He looked up and down: there were no hints of traffic; no sign of further vehicles parked up. The only illumination came from the van's headlamps. He grinned and said, 'What's the problem?'

'Would you mind opening the back?'

'I really don't see the necessity.'

'Just open it,' the man said, voice trembling with subtle menace, 'if you don't mind.' His eyes were shadowed in the gloom.

'I need the key.' Flynn turned and reached back into the cluttered cab. The key was on the dash and, as he lifted it, he placed it between the first and second fingers of his right hand, which he squeezed into a fist so the key protruded solidly between them. He could sense the other man close behind him now, too close; stupidly close as he backed out of the cab, saying, 'Here you are.'

Flynn turned from the waist and hit the man too high, on the side of his face rather than square on the jaw. The key buried itself in his cheek and the man grunted as he fell sideways from the sheer force of the blow, hitting the ground with a meaty crunch. Flynn kicked the man's chin quickly and with as much swing as was possible, stood so close to the idling vehicle, then stepped back and settled into a sideways stance, fists raised, gazing down.

The cop lay still; blood ran from his face and soaked into the powdery earth as if a drink spilled onto the beach. Flynn panted, nauseated suddenly. He reached down and pressed a hand to the man's throat. 'Thought I wouldn't remember?'

He took hold of the cop's wrists and turned him on the scratchy earth. He was heavy and Flynn's hand hurt where the key had pushed against it. He dragged the barely conscious man to the far side and left him leaning against one of the walls, looking at the ink, just to make sure.

Flynn walked back to the cab and turned at a noise to see the fake cop, on his feet, smiling, reaching for his pistol. Flynn drew his own weapon and fired before jumping behind the van. The sound of the shot hung in the air, and then he heard a click as the pistol misfired, then the brush on the far side of the wall crackled and scraped as the fake cop ran. Flynn jumped back into the road, but the man was gone. He swore fiercely and fired two more rounds into the black countryside, frustration driving out his common sense.

He climbed into the cab and drove without looking back. He was safe. Roy was behind this. He checked the wing mirrors as he drove and was relieved when the Casa finally came into view. It was a new building about a hundred yards back from the road leading out of Sant Carles and it looked like a diner, if anything, one of the real crummy ones out the back of petrol stations Flynn had seen countless times along motorways back home. A red sign on top had Casa d'Esclaus written in large white letters across it in the same font as the Coca-Cola logo. Marku waited in front, surrounded by his gang.

Flynn pulled up in front of the building and Marku turned to one of his friends, said something and laughed. He walked over as Flynn climbed out and said, 'You're late.'

'Am I?'

'A joke, you're so serious.' He said something in Romanian to the man closest to him who turned and headed quickly into the building.

'Is Sean around?'

'Why would he be?' Marku asked. His eyes were large and wild and seemed to shine in the light pouring from the door of the building beside him.

Flynn glanced across; the windows on both floors were tinted. The faint sound of music came from within. 'I thought this was his place.'

'Is it?'

'I had that impression.'

Marku held Flynn's gaze for a second too long and then broke into a loud laugh. 'You are serious, too serious. You want a drink?'

The man Marku had sent back into the building returned with four others and they strolled across to the van.

Flynn looked over at them and said, 'No thanks.'

'You have the key?'

'Here.'

'What is this stuff all over it, man?'

'Who knows?'

Marku tapped Flynn's shoulder, hard. 'No trouble?'

'No.'

'That's good,' Marku said, walking over to the van. The

gravel crunched beneath his feet. Two or three cars zipped by, heading home to Sant Carles. 'After the last time,' Marku continued, 'I don't know, let's forget all that now, huh? I'm just glad you got this here and we can make some money.'

'I'll need a lift back into town.'

'Sure, Timofey can take you, no worry.' He gestured to one of the men loitering by the van, a bony shaven-headed youth with a metallic grin. Jesus, Flynn thought, they must come off a production line. 'Now I think you want to see what you have brought, no?'

'I'm not bothered. I just want to get home.'

'No, No, I show you, then you know what all this has been, and it is interesting for you, and for me. I want to see your face.' He smiled again and said something in his own tongue to the man called Timofey who took the key from Marku's proffered hand. 'Come here.'

Flynn stepped closer as the young man pushed the key into the rusting padlock and then, with some difficulty, forced the roller shutter up into the van.

It was the smell first: acid, earthy, the smell of tears. Then the noise: muffled sobs and sickbed groans and then Flynn's sight adjusted to the gloom and he saw at least half a dozen young women crushed against the sides of the van or sprawled over the bed of the truck on three or four soiled single mattresses and a few towels. A skeletal blonde-haired woman looked up, blinking, her eyes dark beneath and he knew she was not looking at him, or anything, too stoned even to know where she was or how she'd got there. Dirt was thick in the girls matted hair. He must have paled as the Romanians began to snigger and Marku pounded his shoulder, overcome by laughter. 'Jesus Christ,' Flynn said, 'what the fuck is this?'

'This,' Marku said, 'is our new venture.'

Flynn turned and walked towards Sant Carles. Marku shouted after him, and the shout became a laugh.

†††

The gate buzzer sounded at half one. Sean frowned, then pulled himself to his feet with some difficulty and walked to the intercom on the wall, one of many dotted throughout the property. The button was hot as a frying pan beneath the pad of his finger. 'Hello.'

'We need to talk.' The cheap speaker strangled the voice.

'I'm out back.' Sean pressed the gate release.

He heard footsteps, hard on the flags, as he walked around the house and then saw Flynn. A fugitive, desperate glow lit his eyes and it looked as though he'd slept in his clothes. The beard was dark across his thin face. He took hold of Sean's sleeve. 'We need to talk.'

'All right, well let me finish this drink…'

'I mean we need to talk.' Flynn's voice was as hard and cold as slate.

Sean's gaze flickered. 'Let's go into the house,' he said.

The two men walked into the gloom of the house and headed for the study where Sean sat behind his desk. He fiddled with the photographs before him. 'I thought I'd better sit down for this,' he said quietly, 'judging by the look on your face.'

'Tell me you didn't know,' Flynn said. He leaned on the

desk, resting his weight on his fists.

'Know what?'

'Know what? About the women in the back of that flaming van, that's what.'

'I did know, of course, I bloody knew, but those girls, none of them had passports or papers or fuck all and we had to get them cross the border somehow.'

'Bullshit! Why get me to drive them from Piera? Fuck Flynn, he can do twenty years, can't he?'

'It wasn't like that. You know the back roads to the farm, that's all, and that psychopath Marku would go down the flaming motorway without a care in the bastard world, that's all boy, nothing sinister.'

'We're in the shit now, Sean; we're talking white slavery....'

'Those girls are willing, so now you're talking shit.'

'...sex trafficking, whatever you want to call it....'

'Shut the fuck up,' Sean shouted, spittle flying from the corners of his mouth. He calmed himself by smoothing the hair at the sides of his head, but his eyes had grown small and vicious. 'You're making me lose my temper now, son, that's all you're doing.'

'I saw them girls,' Flynn said, 'they was hopped up to the fucking eyes, some were even flaming cuffed to each other, don't tell me they came here willing. I ain't an idiot, I know what goes on with them filthy bastards and how they get them women here and what they do, and I don't want any part of it.'

'Listen to me.'

'It's not right!'

'Listen,' Sean continued, his voice steady, as though he were talking a jumper back inside from the window ledge, 'it's not like that, it's like I said: no passports, no papers, that's all. Of course they're gonna look rough when they've been in the back of a wagon for a few hours; done it myself once upon a time going into West Germany, when there still was a West Germany. I guarantee you go back there tonight when we're open for business, and they'll be done up, laughing and joking. Here,' he reached into the desk drawer and Flynn stood back and crossed his arms as Sean placed a thick stack of Euros in front of him. He pushed the money across the desk.

'What's this?'

'Your share.'

'Of what?'

'For what you done,' Sean said, 'for the Casa d'Esclaus, and there'll be more than that.'

Flynn stared at the stack of banknotes and there was a catch at the back of his throat, like the ache before a scream. 'I don't want it; I don't want anything to do with it.'

'Take it,' Sean continued, 'don't grow a conscience now, I know you better than that.'

Flynn reached forward and plucked the money from the table. He held it loosely, as though the notes were made of lead, pulling at his wrist. 'There's something else,' Flynn said, his voice softer now, almost a whisper.

'What's that then?' Sean took a cigar from the desk.

'There was somebody on the road.'

Sean paused. He had struck a match and now his hand hovered before his face, the flame reflecting on the wet surface of his eyes. 'Oh?'

'Dressed up like a cop, only they hadn't bothered to get the transport to go with the shirt, so I suppose they were hoping to blind me with the lights or shock and awe me with the uniform. I saw them before he knew it, tattoos. It was the bloke from the boat.'

Sean had grown very still; only his eyes moved. 'What happened?'

'He won't win any beauty pageants from now on, but he got away.' Flynn pushed the money back across the table. 'They knew I was coming, that's the point. The Stelescus wouldn't know the back roads, so...'

Sean picked the money up without comment and replaced it in his drawer. 'So, who would?'

'Somebody who knows the way we come down from the mountains, someone greedy or stupid; someone who doesn't give a fuck.'

Sean chewed the nail of his thumb and his eyes darted as he spoke. 'Roy?'

'Fucking Roy Quinn.'

'The boys in London are going to have our balls if we don't get their money back.'

'I'm on it.'

A smile split Sean's round, sweat-covered face. 'That's all I want. Revenge for Charlie an' all, God rest him. He was a good bloke, didn't deserve to go the way he did, head blown off like a fucking pheasant.'

Later, and Sean stood in the kitchen of his house, square body enveloped in a late afternoon glow seeping through the window. He held a dart and aimed it with great care at a dartboard suspended on the back of the door, from which two darts, neither placed particularly well, already drooped.

He wore a gown and his thin hair, usually carefully combed and slicked back was messed, as though he had woken from a night of uneasy dreams. His face was blotchy, and there were deep lines beneath his eyes. When he threw the dart, finally, it missed and clattered to the ground and he swore under his breath.

He walked outside where he stood at the top of steps leading down to the pool and breathed in the perfume of the lemon tree. He could see across the plain down to Pineda. The skyline was thick with construction cranes and dust coming from the building sites. He found it hard to believe people could work on sites in such heat. He'd worked in construction for a while, back home, in the '60s. A site down in Bethnal Green and the foreman, a grunting, flat-nosed former soldier, slapped Sean's arm each time he wanted his attention and called him an "'orrible cunt". Sean took it, but the next week, when the insults really began to flow, Sean turned to one of the Irish lads on site and said, 'Give us 'old of that hammer, will yer?' as the foreman was in full flood. He got six months and it was inside that time he met Charlie Hartigan.

The thought of Charlie turned a little in Sean's stomach and he decided to have something a little stronger than tea. He filled a large tumbler with whisky.

He must have fallen asleep because when the buzzer for the gate went it sounded very large in a dream. He was dancing in an old-fashioned dance hall, and it was almost as though the noise of it had reached back to the days when his hair was thick and blond and there was only cunning in his eyes to betray his true nature.

The sun was very low now, almost behind the pines. Cicadas twittered somewhere in the wasteland between his house and the road. 'What you forgot Flynn?' He said into a machine on the wall.

A man's voice, 'Are you going to let me in or am I waiting out here all the night?'

Cezar Stelescu; even through a tinny intercom, he sounded like a murderer. There was a completely dead, careless emptiness to his voice, like the wind blowing through the burned-out wreck of a car.

Sean pressed the buzzer and walked through the house to the front door, which he opened as he fastened his robe. He swallowed as a dark car pulled up onto white gravel and the two brothers climbed out. There would be four of them in London, Sean thought, a couple of heavies to watch the head blokes; but the Stelescus did not feel the need for minders and it was this confidence, running through them like lead through a rubber cosh, that got to him.

Sean, his mind working, turned on his professional smile and rushed outside. His carpet slippers slapped on the dirty ground. 'Cezar, my friend, how nice to see you; come in lads and have a drink; business good?'

'The same as always,' Cezar said. He was sixty years old, with a long, sallow face and serious peasant eyes that always seemed at the edge of tears. He wore a long moustache and his lips barely moved when he spoke. 'The farm is ideal.'

Marku stood behind his brother, smoking a cigarette. He wore a flashy tracksuit and trainers and played with a gold ring in his ear as he listened, as he had his entire life, to his brother's voice.

'You're welcome to it,' Sean said, leading the way through the house and out to the pool, 'place only has bad memories for me.'

'Come now,' Cezar said, 'you have a share of the profits.'

'But not yet, do I?'

'Soon,' Cezar said. He walked over to the bar and poured himself a glass of vodka. 'I have to account for this loss to some very dangerous men. I'm only glad we have worked it out. You have ice?'

'Underneath,' Sean said. His throat had gone dry. 'Which men are these?'

'The men who gave me the money I had to pay back.' He pointed at Sean. 'Which you have to pay back, as one of your men "sold us out".' He smiled. 'You saved your life, Mr. Mallon, making this deal with us. Not from me, you understand I wish you no harm, but the people who gave me the money; they do not take mistakes lightly.' He drank and looked around the garden with a singularly bored expression. 'This is good vodka; where was I?'

'Saving lives, Cezar.'

'This is right,' he said, glancing across at Marku, who was touching the lemons on the tree and smelling them. 'But you cannot save a traitor.'

'We don't know who robbed us yet' Sean said. 'I have my best blokes looking for 'im right now. There's this fella, Roy.' He caught the look Cezar gave his brother. 'Is something wrong?'

'Quinn?'

'Yeah,' Sean said.

Cezar walked to the edge of the pool. 'We already know who your Judas is, that is no longer something you need to,' he turned, smiling and thought for the most suitable expression, 'lose sleep over.'

Sean paled a little as he struggled for the best thing to do or say. 'Well, are you going to let me know?'

Cezar walked across to the pool and stared into the water. 'How well do you trust Flynn?'

'I trust him,' Sean said sharply.

Cezar shrugged and said something in Romanian to his brother who winked at Sean as he walked back through the house. Cezar waited until he heard the door close and turned to Sean. 'My brother,' he said, 'is a dog that hates a leash and I am finding it more and more difficult to control him. I do not wish to share everything with him, not just yet.' He shrugged his broad shoulders and said, 'Flynn; Marku will collect him from outside the tower at Esquirol, six o'clock, take him for a drive and we will settle this matter finally. Then,' he walked across to the bar and set the glass on the bamboo top, 'we have all of our pieces back to the beginning of the game, you and I.'

'Flynn is my number one,' Sean said, his voice faltering a little at the edges. He felt a tingle of nausea in his stomach, his gown had blown open, and he had not noticed. His body was red and sunburned in the last of the afternoon's light.

'Perhaps,' Cezar said, 'but he was also on the boat. Why kill Charlie and not him?' He crossed to the door of the house and motioned for Sean to join him. 'Six o'clock, arrange it for me. In the meantime, I want to discuss Casa d'Esclaus;

there are one or two things I want you to know.'

†††

Sean watched the gates close after their car and closed his eyes. He walked back into the house. His mobile lay on the tile-topped kitchen table and he started to tap Flynn's number into it. 'It would appear your luck has run out,' he said.

†††

Flynn took a cab to Esquirol beach and walked to the tower that was set like a headstone against the coming night. There was the empty atmosphere that comes with dusk beside the Mediterranean. Flynn stood beside the tower and looked out to sea. He was aware of the first touches of anxiety biting into his stomach and wrapping around his chest like a lifejacket several sizes too small, and then the first shivers, small electric touches in his shoulders, beneath the blades, shaking in spite of himself. He heard the car before he saw it, the engine punching through the calm. He pushed himself from the wall of the tower. It was a small red "muscle" car, coming much too quickly from Pineda; the driver hit the brakes and raised a mushroom cloud of sand blown up from the beach. Marku Stelescu wound the window down and smiled. He listened to some kind of wailing dance music with an insistent beat and smiled with every one of his shark's teeth. His hair was tight against his skull. 'Hola!' He shouted, high, 'How much for the night?'

Flynn ignored what he said. 'Sean says you wanted to see

me?'

'I do, I do,' he sniffed, 'we're going to go for a drive, you and me.' He looked at Flynn for what seemed a long time. The engine growled like an empty stomach and there was a strange knocking sound from somewhere beneath the vehicle. 'So?' 'So what?'

'Are you going to get the fuck in or what?' The smile dropped and revealed, briefly, the real man behind the eyes.

Flynn looked left and right and then climbed in. The car was new and had the sharp plastic smell of fresh upholstery; Marku turned to him and gestured towards the seatbelt hanging beside the door. 'Better to be safe than sorry,' he said, removing his glasses and grinning.

They drove through the country without conversation. Flynn watched the land through his window unreel like a movie: olive trees spaced widely on slopes leading to the mountains; low walls, ochre rocks stacked like stale loaves in slanting light. Flynn held onto himself very tightly as they drove.

Marku pulled the car up at a building site. The engine's heat flooded through the car and Marku sighed, 'We are here.'

'Where's here?'

'A place,' Marku said, 'as good as any; they were building a swimming pool here but ran out of money, now it is empty, abandoned.'

'You're a strange lad, Marku,' Flynn said, sitting very still and looking at the dried cement splashed across the side of a truck and the piled bricks and an excavator like a hulking dinosaur beneath three tall pines that cast a shadow across the scrub. Marku climbed out of the car, motioning for Flynn to do likewise.

There was a dog barking somewhere and the constant trickling, dreamlike noise of cicadas. Marku walked to the rear of the car, lifted his zippered top at the back and dragged a pistol out of his belt.

Flynn stared at the pistol as though he didn't know what it was. The loose white shirt blew around his waist in a dry breeze that came across the plain, 'Fuck,' he whispered.

The young man grinned and held the weapon before him as though testing the weight. The wind was high in the three pines and rustled a plastic bag against the wire fence and it felt to Flynn as though that dry, dead mortuary wind was all that existed now.

'Beautiful, isn't it,' Marku said, lifting the pistol to his nose and inhaling deeply as though it was a rose, 'it's Russian, a Stechkin; they made these for KGB; it does not jump when you fire; look at this.' He drew a silencer from his pocket. The pistol had a tubular steel nose extending forward from the top slider, to which Marku attached the silencer, doubling the weapon's length, so it hung from his hand, long, shining, looked after, but an old gun, not quite an antique. Flynn watched as though it was a cobra. 'A range of 25 metres; 3 or 4 rounds a burst in full automatic. I love this gun; it has always been a good friend. You can get a shoulder stock, but I lost it in Sofia, I think, but the silencer?' He smiled. 'Man, I love this gun.'

'It's very handsome,' Flynn said in a thick voice. His mouth was unbelievably dry; he hadn't known it was possible for a mouth to become so arid.

'My brother and me,' Marku began, 'have wondered for a

long time what happened with the boat, you know; we have had problems because of this, we lost much, and our names are not what they were; people talk; they think we are too stupid to find the thieves, or else too weak to deal with them.' He smiled. 'But I am going to show them how the Stelescu family deals with thieves.'

'But you don't know who it was.'

'We know.' He said this with great deliberation, dropping each word into the silence as stones drop into a calm pool of dark water.

They stood regarding each other through the harsh flaring light flooding from the sunset, and then Marku said, 'So let's do this.'

Flynn closed his eyes, waited, and heard the metallic accent of the pistol cocking and then Marku opened the boot of the car and Flynn heard a muffled sob and the suspension grinding as the weight it carried shifted. He opened his eyes and saw Marku at the rear of the car, swearing in his own language, then looking over and growling, 'Help me then, motherfucker; I can't lift with one hand.'

Flynn dashed across, his boot heels crunching in the dust; there was a man, wrists bound behind his back with yellow plasticuffs, a scratchy brown hessian sack that looked damp in places across his face. Marku, holding the man's ankle, had dragged him halfway out of the car with one hand. He gestured with the pistol at the man's other leg and, with a scornful expression, said, 'Get him out of my fucking car.'

Flynn pulled the man's leg, lifting him; the man wore trousers that were wetly dark along the front of the thighs and he was sobbing.

'Quickly,' Marku puffed, his face slick with sweat, leaving the task to Flynn, 'he's pissed his pants and this car is new and I don't want it to stink.' He wiped his face with his sleeve, arm weighted by the pistol. 'I am meeting a girl later.'

The man fell to his knees in the gravel and Marku stepped across and pulled the sacking from his head as though unveiling a work of art. The man glanced down and then up and his eyes looked as though somebody had rubbed pepper into them. Flynn felt a churning in his stomach and his throat palpated with the rising of his heart. It was Roy.

'Buenos tardes,' Marku said, mockingly, 'you piece of shit.'

There was plumber's tape across Roy's mouth and the edge of it cut against his septum; it was very tight and his cheeks bulged across it; a stream of blood and snot stained the shiny white web of the fabric. Pieces of fluff were stuck into his greasy hair and his red eyes turned to Flynn. He tried to speak through the tape, and Marku hushed him, waving a finger in front of his face. 'I'm not going to take this tape off,' he said. 'I do not like to hear a man beg and cry and pray.' He turned to Flynn. 'You wouldn't beg, would you? You're like me; you wouldn't plead, or pray to gods who are not there. You'd take it.' He nodded, more to himself than anything. 'But this putoi? He'd weep like a woman.'

'How,' Flynn stammered, ignoring the nausea rampaging through his body, trying not to let a note of fear sound on his tongue, 'how do you know Roy had anything to do with this?'

'Because he could not keep hold of his tongue,' Marku said, 'because he was too greedy and too foolish; because he hated you, my friend, and had to tell the world that he had struck against you.'

Flynn scowled. 'Who says this?'

'This motherfucker was even on the boat that night,' Marku said, 'he told a woman who told me; trying to make himself a man; he was a boxer, in older days, was he not?' Flynn nodded. 'And there was still enough strength in his arm to knock you cold. He told everybody.'

'I need to hear this from him.'

'He will only cry again.'

'Roy?' Flynn kneeled in the dust beside the man, trying not to look into his frightened, streaming eyes. 'Is this true?' Flynn dragged his finger in the dust, carving a shape, idly.

The young man nodded, struggling to make the motion clear because his head was trembling violently.

Flynn inhaled slowly and deeply and closed his eyes. He turned to Marku, and said, 'We need to find out who the others were and maybe we can get back our stuff? I need the other blokes.'

'We only need this one.'

'I don't see why.'

'Because this stupid bastard had the coke hidden in his apartment,' Marku sniffed, 'and we have our deal back on the table.'

Flynn turned. 'So what are we going to do?'

'This.'

The crack of the silenced pistol was sharp and pure against the noiseless heaviness of the plain. The back of Roy Quinn's skull came away in a single coughing vomit of bone and the gelatinous scarlet of the brain and a crimson vapour showered forward across the white linen of Flynn's shirt; microscopic dots, like spray from a toothbrush, speckled his sleeve.

Marku hadn't paused to aim, simply lifted his arm and fired. It was a good shot, Flynn thought, considering.

The young man's body fell back into the ditch and a dark pool of blood ran into the powdery dust with unbelievable speed.

Marku began to unscrew the silencer, gazing down at the body with dark, mournful eyes as he worked at the pistol, then, almost as an afterthought, he walked across and spat on the ground. He swore gently and looked over at Flynn, still on his knees, close to the ditch. The air filled with the rank smell of a body loosing itself, the acidic, copper and open sewer smell of murder.

Flynn spoke over his shoulder, 'There was no need.'

'He's dead,' Marku said, 'let's go.'

'We needed him.'

'It doesn't matter now,' Marku said, 'leave him to Hell. Come on.' He slapped a hand on Flynn's shoulder. 'I know now we can trust you.'

Flynn raised his head; his eyes were heavy and he was tired, deeply tired and didn't know if there was strength in his knees to lift him. The red stains across his shirt had started to run into each other and he was aware of it all; the sky, the feel of the earth, the perfume of the settling dust and the pistol, the scrunch of Stelescu's trainers as he walked to the car. As always in the presence of a dead man, he wondered what exactly the world had just lost and felt the strange privilege that embarrassed him always of being for some reason still alive.

They left Roy where he had fallen; legs twisted, like a broken toy, the dust around him heavy with the drying and congealing blood like the sand in a ring after they have dragged out the dead bull. One leg of his trousers had worked up around his calf and the flesh was harshly pale in the twilight like the skin of a joint of pork; the image barged into Flynn's heart and he could not rid himself of it. His thighs trembled and he did not know how they carried him back to the car. Marku, in already and sat behind the wheel, lit a cigarette and offered one to Flynn, which he took. He sighed, the other man held the gas lighter between them, Flynn leaned forward, and the dried tobacco crackled in the immense quiet of the space between them. 'You don't like that I kill this man?'

Flynn shrugged. 'I would have liked to talk with him,' he said, 'that is all.'

'You don't look well, Flynn; I'm surprised.'

'A bloke doesn't have to get used to it,' Flynn said, quietly, sucking on the cigarette.

'Let's go,' Marku sounded disappointed, as though he had expected something other, as though a game had been ruined.

†††

They drove back into Sant Carles through the new fall of the night and Flynn was dropped off on the Passeig Miramar. Marku tried to smile, but he could not even pretend at happiness. He left Flynn beside the fishermen's sheds and the working pier and headed at great speed in the direction of Pineda.

Flynn walked to the edge of the pier, looked out over the fishing boats, and heard the jangle of their ties and stays and

the wind curling over the ripples of the dark heavy water.
He called Sean's mobile. His hands no longer shook, but it
was there, at the back of his throat, the shaved steel taste of
fear. 'Flynn?' Sean's voice was high, concerned, perhaps even
a little shocked. 'What's up? How did it go?'

'They killed Roy.'

'He's dead?'

Flynn walked to the edge and looked down into the water.
It was starting to get cold. His shirt was dark and dry now
and he stared balefully at the spatter marks as he said, 'Dead
as he can be.'

'Shit,' Sean said, 'where is he right now?'

'In the backcountry.'

'They left him?'

'Making a point.'

'Where are you?'

'Sant Carles, he just dropped me off.'

Flynn closed his eyes; he needed a drink. Half a dozen
men worked on one of the boats close to him, throwing the
plastic fish boxes up onto the concrete pier and telling a joke
in a flat, musical Catalan.

It sounded as though Sean had the mobile phone jammed
against his jaw. 'Case closed, I suppose.'

'There's still this tattooed guy.'

'He'll be long gone.'

The phone clicked and fell silent. Flynn leaned against
the steel fence surrounding the fish quay and breathed out,
slowly and deeply.

He lit a cigarette hoping to take away the high end of his
nerves. An elderly couple passed. The man glanced down at

Flynn's stained sleeve and then looked away quickly.

It was like being in a shark cage, surrounded by monsters, safe only so long as you had faith in the thin bars, but the cage was an illusion, he saw that now, and his heart was open to their teeth.

He thought of Roy, blood running like oil from a crashed car. He'd seen it before and he would see it again, no doubt, but he knew a man should not take another away like that; it was against something powerful that stood behind the world and that he felt sometimes, in the dark of the night.

Gareth Spark's *short fiction and poetry has appeared in Shotgun Honey, Line Zero, Ink, sweat and tears, Out of the Gutter, Line Zero and Deepwater Literary Review, among others. He is the author of the poetry collection "Rain in a dry land" (Mudfog Press, 2008) and is currently working on a novel.*
   He lives in Whitby, Yorkshire.